My Favourite Person

Cheeky Chums, Furry Friends & Fantastic Family

Edited by Aimée Vanstone & Donna Samworth

First published in Great Britain in 2010 by:

Young Writers

Young Writers
Remus House
Coltsfoot Drive
Peterborough
PE2 9JX
Telephone: 01733 890066
Website: www.youngwriters.co.uk

Foreword

Our 'My Favourite Person 2009' poetry competition attracted young aspiring poets to show their admiration for those who have made an impact in their life. What better way to let those closest know how much they are appreciated.

We are delighted to present this thoughtful collection. After reading through the hundreds of entries it is clear the amount of enthusiasm and love that went into writing these poems, therefore we hope you'll agree they are an inspiring and heart-warming read.

Young Writers was established in 1991 to promote poetry and creative writing to schoolchildren and encourage them to read, write and enjoy it. Here at Young Writers we are sure you'll agree that this special edition achieves our aim and celebrates today's wealth of young writing talent. We hope you enjoy this anthology for many years to come.

Contents

The Poems

The King Of Pop

I know a lot of people,
Who have the gift of a great voice,
But, to pick my favourite,
There is really only one choice.

Michael Jackson is my hero,
A legend of all time,
The talent enriched within him
Shone through him in his prime.

I may not have met him,
But the mark he left upon my heart,
The memory of his greatness,
Will never grow apart.

They called him the king of pop,
It was more than just a name,
It was respect for what he was capable of,
The reason for his fame.

Dance is shown through many ways,
With practise and perfection,
When my hero showed his way of dance,
He gave it a whole new definition.

His songs were more than just words,
More than just carrying a tune,
He really hoped that the world,
Would come to its senses soon.

He wowed me, he amazed me,
He stuck by what he had to say,
But topping all these things,
He taught me being different was OK.

So even though this great man
Is not with us today,
In our hearts he will remain,
His memories will never drift away.

Nirshika Vimalnath (12)

My Baby Sister

My baby sister
Is so cute
Her mouth is big
But her heart is too.

I love her dearly
And I'm sure she knows
Although I tease her
My love for her grows.

When she's happy
She is all playful
Running around
It makes her cheerful.

When she's sad
She gets in a strop
She sits in one place
And she doesn't get up.

When she doesn't
Get her way
She stomps around
And tries to run away.

She sucks her thumb
Day in, day out
And she gets angry
When you tell her to take it out.

She always sticks
Around with my mum
Especially when
She's having a tantrum.

And then at night
She'll cry and weep
Just because
She wants to sleep.

My baby sister
Is so cute
Her mouth is big
But her heart is too.

Hema Joshi (11)

For That Special Someone

This poem is a dedication to you,
It is for everything you say and everything you do.
You're more greater than the best works of music and masterpieces of art.
So, you must know you have a special place in my heart.
You are so unique and without you the family would crash and burn
and fall apart.
Like the flowers you blossom and bring colour into my days,
I love you so much like a horse loves hay.
You're an all-singing, all-dancing parent, after all you're more than just okay.
I have begun to realise you are irreplaceable,
Like the sun you are vital and without you I'd be lost.
The more and more I think about it I'm surprised you don't come with a cost.
Since you are a diamond and therefore rare.
You always go that extra mile and I can see you truly care.
You are fantastic in your own right
There amongst the other stars glistening bright.
Not mentioning that I appreciate all that you do:
The delicious cooking; the cleaning and washing up too!
You treat me really kindly and there is no space for the things you buy me.
You spoil me rotten and when things are bad
You make them soften and all's forgotten.
This poem may be rubbish as I'm not good with words
But the love I feel for you is higher than the buildings, trees and birds.
You are simply the epitome of great,
You lighten up a room even if you turn up late.
Nevertheless, you are extremely funny
And are someone that is always remembered and admired from afar.
Having said that, you know who you are . . .

Shelley Sharma (15)

My Favourite Person

My favourite person, who can it be?
My favourite person, who is that to me?
Someone I know? It could be a friend,
Or someone famous? The list has no end!
Are they in my family? Someone I've not met?
Is it a teacher? Or even my pet?

As I'm thinking, my mum comes in,
With a cup of cocoa and biscuits in a tin.
Suddenly a thought comes to my mind,
Indeed my mum is very kind.
That's the answer! It's my mum,
The one who stops me from feeling glum!

Day in, day out, she's always there,
Till the end she will care.
She's always here to help me out,
Without her I would scream and shout.
She joins in when I'm playing a game,
When she's away, home's not the same.

Together we have a lot of fun,
Especially when there's plenty of sun.
When we're having a picnic at the park,
She keeps me safe, even in the dark.
I like it when we go to the fair,
My mum and me, we make a good pair.

For bringing me up I owe her a lot,
She's given me everything I have got!
My awesome mum means the world to me,
There's no one like her and could never be.
The one who's always filled my tummy,
My favourite person is my mummy!

Mohammad Shoaib (10)

My Mum

My lovely mum
She's a lot of fun
She's pretty and smart
And has a good heart
Her cooking is nice
Just perfect with spice
She keeps the house clean
She's such a pretty queen
She is very, very pretty
And loves London city
She is very kind
And looks so divine
Her skin is chocolate-brown
She's the queen wearing a crown
She's as sweet as a rose
And wears pretty clothes
She is as sweet as honey
Her food fills my tummy
She makes me smile
She has great style
She's filled with love
As pretty as a dove
She's a very glamorous girl
Who likes diamonds and pearls
She smells of sweet perfume
She's a beautiful bride married to a groom
My mum is the most amazing thing
Like the first day of spring
My mum is the best
And has a big heart in her chest.

Lauren Robinson (11)

My Favourite Person

You stand out from the rest
You really are the best
You stand out
From all the other people
You don't stand about
Or prick me with a needle
Whatever you do
You keep me smiling
And make me laugh
When I'm worried or whining
Whenever you're around
The place gets brighter
If I'm lost in the dark
You're my lighter
You're always there
To give me a hug
And to give me hot chocolate
In your special mug
You're always there
To give me confidence
To cheer me on
And when there's a problem
You raise me up and take care of me
Give me shelter and a family
You make sure I am safe
As I grow up you give me faith
My favourite person is my mum
Whatever I need she gets it done
I wouldn't be so happy if it wasn't for the things you do
I feel so lucky with a mum like you!

Jessica Lai (12)

My Best Schoolmate, Marcus

My mate Marcus is a friendly lad,
With him I always enjoy a chat.
Brown eyes, ginger hair,
Tall and tough,
But not a bit rough.
He's a boy, I'm a girl
But we don't care.

I'm beating the rest,
I notice Marcus drawing stickmen,
Even though it's a test.
He's a boy, I'm a girl
But we don't care.

A time in Class 1
We were drawing postcards,
It was so much fun,
Then we had to give it away
Either to a friend or family.
Marcus gave his to me
And I gave mine to him.

Friends so long
We hope it won't end now.
Future's going to be hard
But we will stick together,
Small school to secondary school,
We don't care,
As long as we both go there.

Caitlin Fotheringham (10)

My Mum

She's a . . .
Fashion dresser,
My impresser,
Make-up wearer,
Is my carer,
Fight stopper,
Drink popper,
Up late,
Always great,
Cuddle monster,
Hates lobster,
Fab cooker,
Lovely looker,
Tear mender,
Money spender,
My personal driver,
Has a spare fiver,
My tumble dryer,
Puts out my fire,
Loves me lots,
Gets rid of my spots,
Giraffe lover,
Lovely mother,
She's my chum,
Not dumb,
Never glum,
My mum!

Poppy Hellaby (11)

My Brother, Matthew - Haiku

He is really great
He is a cheerful playmate
He is my brother.

James MacLeod (11)

My Friend, Sunnie

A special pony came to stay
One bright September day
All he did was call and neigh
For me to go to his field and play.

His chestnut coat
Flaxen mane and tail
Magnificent behind
Our post and rail!

My mother says he's a little bug
Er, what's that he's doing to his rug?

Welsh mountain pony
Section C
One day a champion
He will be!

Saddle and bridle gleaming bright
Had I worked hard last Saturday night
Sunday morning plaits in tight
At the show we did alright.

He cost Mum and Dad
A lot of money
Worth every penny
My pony called Sunnie.

Sunnie, he's my very best friend
Together we will be, till the very end.

Hollie-Ann Pearson (11)

My Favourite Person!

My favourite person is my mum,
When I'm naughty she says I'm a pain in the bum.
My mum knows how to have fun,
Guess what? . . . I love my mum!

Charlotte Marshall-Neale (11)

My Favourite Person 2009

My favourite person is my older brother.
He is not ordinary, special in a strange way.
He pushes, he pinches, he pokes
and is
remarkably good at annoying.
He can sit there all day just calling me names,
but if he weren't there I'd miss him.

He is quite unpredictable if a Chelsea match is on.
He'll be forever over the moon
or
in a turtle's shell.
He wishes to become like Didier Drogba soon.
Sometimes I wonder what the house
would sound like without him.
I'd miss him.

So all of the things you've heard
and
a dozen more to come.
I adore him to bits,
so without him a chunk of my heart
would be missing.

Although I do wonder
what the house would sound like without
him
Maybe a lot more *peaceful* . . .

Maanya Suri (8)

Mum

M um is the best, better than the rest
U are cooler than all the rest
M um you shine like a star
M um you're the best mum to ever live
Y ou're the best mum in the world!

Aimee Wetherick (10)

Daddy

My daddy is the best,
You can put him to the test.

His stories are so animated, they come alive,
He taught me swimming, now he's teaching me to dive.

We go on outings, for bicycle rides together,
We collect on our way wild flowers, curious fossils, fluffy feathers.

When I get nightmares, I go and snuggle up to him,
He comforts me and whispers, 'Don't worry, it was only a dream.'

When I make mistakes and I'm in very big trouble,
He readily forgives me and says, 'Let's burst it together, it is just a bubble.'

His jokes are really funny, they always make me laugh,
If there was a chart for the funniest people, he'd be at the top of the graph.

Be it difficult sums, or spellings that are extremely hard,
There is nothing he can't solve, sometimes I think he's a wizard!

Be it toys in a shop window, or books, even a tabby cat,
I only have to think, 'I want it,' and he gets it for me just like that.

He's always been an audience to all my performances,
He stands behind the finishing line and cheers me on at the school races.

When I'm playing Chinese checkers or some other board game with him,
He loses every time on purpose and somehow always makes me win.

I know however big I grow or whatever in my life I do,
My dad will always love me lots and I will love him too.

Oly Ganguly (8)

Boo (My Brother)

Boo is my brother, he plays football all about,
He normally plays it when I'm out and about.
He watches it every day and never listens to me,
When my mum says, 'Olivia and Boo it's time for tea,'
He still keeps watching it and he still doesn't listen to me.

Olivia Schofield (8)

The King Of Pop - R.I.P - Michael Jackson

This person is a legend
But sadly is dead
He did so many amazing things
That we will never forget

Like giving to charity
And creating his own
Send messages through his music
On stage through the microphone

Though he has been through troubles
It didn't stop him
From carrying on his dream
To fulfilling his destiny

The message he sent
Through his microphone
Was to heal the world
And to help those with no home

To stop all this war
To spread the word
To love the children
To show them you care

His music is loved
From whatever age
Although he is dead
The King of Pop will always remain.

Shahela Kodabuckus (15)

Dedication To Oscar

O scar is my best friend, the Newfoundland dog
S adly passed away just last week, was
C ute, cuddly and caring
A dorable, very big, extremely naughty and mischievous
R est in peace my best friend Oscar.

Emma Burns (9)

Special People

I know a lot of people,
I love them all the same,
My mother does a lot for me,
My friends can play a game.

My family are there for me,
To hold me when I'm sad,
Love you can always count on,
For that I'm really glad.

The people who I live with,
Although they sometimes moan,
They always say goodbye to me wherever I may roam,
They always come to greet me whenever I come home.

Sometimes people disagree,
Over silly things, why could that be?
Not everyone can feel the same,
Forgive and forget, that's what I say!

So my favourite person,
I regret to say,
A hard question, be that as it may,
Because everyone's special in their own unique way.

My conclusion may not satisfy,
It may not be good for you or I,
If in a single clear answer I had to confide,
I truthfully certainly couldn't decide.

Jacob Charles (11)

My Friend Amber

A lways friendly no matter what the situation
M ad about food
B rilliant at squeaking
E xpert at chilling out
R eally she is a great guinea pig!

Sophia Clark (8)

13

Guess Who My Favourite Person Is?

I am so lovely, oh yes I am,
I've always been super, even in the pram.
I am so pretty, sweet as ice cream,
I am a beauty with the grace of a queen.

I am so clever, I'm a real brainbox,
I am so cunning, wise as a fox.
I am a great cook, I was born to bake,
In just a minute I can whip up a cake.

I am a songbird, I sound so sweet,
If you're around, it's an unforgettable treat.
I am so active, I teach a swimming course,
I am so strong, I can carry a milkman and a horse.

Another Oscar, oh what a bore,
That's the twelfth one, how many more?
My hair is so shiny, like the iridescent stars,
They even love me on Planet Mars.

I am a genius, university at three,
They said I was too clever, so I went home for tea.
I discovered Saturn one sunny Saturday,
Whilst drinking tea with the president of the USA.

I am so different, I made the chocolate bar,
Oh yes, and the Ferrari car.
Who is this angel? Who could it be?
Who's my favourite person? Oh, it's lovely me!

Scarlet Wood (10)

My Special Friend

You have to be rather lucky
to have a special friend like mine
I never feel really lonely
'cause she's there for me all the time.

My best friend is never nasty
She never leaves me out
of games that we love to play
She's a friend without a doubt.

She's kind and caring
thoughtful, fun
Joyful and lively
when we play in the sun.

She's never boastful
never mad
She cheers me up
when I am sad.

My best friend is clever
the smartest in the class
She knows the answer to everything
and in exams she's sure to pass.

This poem is all about
my wonderful favourite friend
Hope you all enjoyed it
now it comes to an end.

Kirsty King (9)

Mum

I love you Mum,
You're the best,
You're that good,
You'll beat the rest,

You hold the key,
To all the food,
When you finish cooking,
I'm in a great mood,

When I'm scared Mum,
You hold me tight,
You're the shield,
So I'm alright,

Mum, Mum,
You're fashion mad,
But when it comes to football,
You're football sad,

You got me to the world Mum,
You taught me how to walk,
You're always on my side,
You also taught me how to talk,

I love you Mum,
You're the best,
You're that good,
You'll beat the rest.

Mohammed Sanuwar Hussain (10)

My Gran

I have more than one person I love,
Writing about them would not be enough,
But there is one person whom I am a fan,
And that special person is my gran.

My gran's always there in times of need,
When I am naughty, she doesn't get peeved,
When I was young she was making my nappy,
Now I am older she still makes me happy.

My gran is beautiful inside and out,
She never brings me the slightest of doubt,
Her cooking is guaranteed to be great,
Having her as my grandma has had to be fate!

My gran doesn't look after me, not all of the time,
She has my auntie and grandad to mind,
She cooks my aunt's dinner, whilst my grandad sings,
My aunt goes travelling, brings back magnets and things.

I have a young sister and she is great,
I say, 'Mum and Dad, she's my mini best mate!'
So when they're hardworking and my sister's at school,
My gran picks her up all year round and past fall.

So . . . I've told you now why I love my gran,
Anything you ask her she says, 'Yes, I can!'
And when she's gone and I'm still here,
She will be in my dreams and I won't shed a tear.

Sadie Fox (12)

My Tessy

This person's a girl,
She's got lots of curls,
Her name isn't Betty,
But for sure, my Tessy.

She isn't a trickster,
She's my teenage sister.
Her name isn't Betty,
But for sure, my Tessy.

She buys me some sweets,
She walks on two feet.
Her name isn't Betty,
But for sure, my Tessy.

She makes me cry,
She acts very sly.
Her name isn't Betty,
But for sure, my Tessy.

She's cool, she's fun,
She acts like my mum.
Her name isn't Betty,
But for sure, my Tessy.

She's my new best friend,
She has the new trend.
Her name isn't Betty,
But for sure, *my Tessy!*

Roxanna Yarf-Abbasi (11)

A Special Friend . . .

A friend like you
Is hard to find.
Sometimes we argue
But never mind.

You make me laugh
And make me smile,
Keeping me happy,
That's your style.

Together we both
Reach the skies,
Because our friendship
Is very wise.

You live inside me,
In my heart
Like a special
Piece of art.

Despite all the fun
And all the laughter,
Our friendship will last
Forever and after.

We were always
And will yet be
The bestest friends,
You and me.

Sadia Akram (11)

My Favourite Person

My favourite person is in my mind,
So sweet, so gentle and kind,
She helps me through tough,
and pours my cereal until I've had enough,
She kisses me goodnight and gives me a hug,
and protects me from a dangerous thug,
She says I'm a guardian angel giving good luck,
and she gives me money, at school, for tuck,
She gives me presents when I'm good,
even when I can't be more good, she says I could,
She loves me to the sun and back,
and carries a bundle of love in a sack,
She hands it out to me with a smile,
While looking for more through a file,
With a blink of an eye I'm in her arms,
don't care about anything, not even the alarms,
me feeling special throughout the day,
it makes me want to say,
'I love you so much!'
especially when we touch,
I can feel the love deep down,
I feel like a queen, with a crown,
She's the person you can guess,
better than the rest,
I was in her tummy,
my very own mummy!

Samantha Viggars (11)

My Mum

My mum is always there for me
She buzzes around like a bee
Because she cares so much about me
When I was four
I played with my toys on the floor
While I grow up my mum's beside me
She'll try to be the best she can be
Young girls have many dreams
Falling more than once can cause hundreds of screams
When I'm sad and I cry
I feel so in the dark I'll die
Then my mum comes to my rescue
No one in this world, not even you
Can have a better mum than me
She taught me my ABC
From baby clothes to popular style
When she's with me I always smile
My mum is my hero
Even when I was zero
The food she makes is always yum
She's not just my mum
She's my best friend
Till the very end
This poem is almost done
And she is my favourite person
My mum.

Eileidh Greig (13)

My Mum

I love my mum to pieces,
She's such a beautiful sight,
Even if you make her mad,
She'll never give you a fright.

With her eyes as pure as gold,
And a smile brighter than my day,
Who could ask for a better mum,
Who who, I say?

My mum's such a star,
Her heart is as big as a car,
But a car can't go that far.

My mum she is the best,
She's better than the rest,
My mum she loves her tea,
Almost as much as me.

My mum is the best,
But sometimes needs a rest,
So Mum, settle down,
There's no need to frown.

So now it's time for bed,
To rest your sleepy head,
Tomorrow will be another day,
To giggle, laugh and play!

Georgia Bicknell (11)

My Mum . . .

She is the best mum because she takes me to football every week
and cheers me on.

She looks after me really well.

She's with me every step of the way.

That is why my mum is the best.

Thomas Taylor (10)

The Impossible Made Possible

I never knew it was possible
to get a sister so much more,
I never knew it was possible
well, until I was four.
She's more than a sister
she's the best friend,
that you can expect
to have till the end.

Whether it's day or
whether it's dawn,
I knew she was there
since she was born.
When I cry
she starts to cry,
and when I laugh
you know why.

So in return
I'm there for thee,
in Heaven or Earth
where she may be.
Yes, now you know
life's a puzzle,
that something impossible
can be made possible!

Ada Onyiuke (10)

My Favourite Person

My favourite person is my sister, Jemma.
She is one and has learnt to run.
We play together outdoors
And in some games I even let Jemma win.
When we go to bed at night,
We snuggle up tight and say goodnight.

Louise McElroy (7)

Nikey

A few years back, but not long ago,
A newborn cat was put up for show.
The Leicester Mercury stated on the advertisement page,
To visit the house and save up my wage.
I entered the house not sure what to expect,
Until it caught my attention, he was almost perfect,
His emerald-green, sparkling eyes
Wandered around searching for flies,
I took a step closer and admired his size,
In comparison to the cardboard box he was just a pair of eyes,
He wasn't brown and he wasn't black,
Nor was he white, ginger or fat,
The woman said he was tabby but not to me,
I saw him as cute, angelic and free,
Streaks of spicy cinnamon-brown,
Hidden amongst royal-gold you'd find on a crown,
His mischievous face made him unique,
Distinguished him from the others, like a dog with a beak,
But that's not quite right because he didn't seem weird,
Just carefree and fresh, there was nothing he feared,
I knew straight away he was perfect for me,
So I took him home and now he's three,
Of course I still love him, he's my adorable cat,
It's just every so often a dead mouse lies on my mat!

Hafsah Ali (15)

My Friend Bethan

B eing silly is her thing
E xcitable, bubbly, full of zing
T alkative, chatty, a tune to sing
H appy, smiley, never dull
A nxious, curious, willing to help
N aughty,cheeky, full of fun

My friend Bethan is number one!

Lucy Brundish (10)

24

Somebody Special!

My mum is the best daughter,
Best mother and best friend.
My mum is a person
Whose love never ends.
My mum is somebody
Who looks out for others.
My mum is the most sweet
And one-of-a-kind mother!
My mum is reliable
And treats people with respect.
My mum is full of surprises,
You never know what to expect next!
My mum is kind and generous,
Always gracious and grateful.
My mum is extremely gentle,
For she is always cared for.
She never really smacks us,
Maybe just a few shouts,
Really fun and outgoing,
That's what my mum's about.
My mum is much more than
My dad, my sister or my brother.
My mum is a mum
That's like no other.

Fahima Haque (11)

Finley, My Favourite Person

F unny as a clown, that's my friend Finley
I like it when he plays tag with me
N othing makes me happier than playing with Finley
L aughing all the time when we are together
E very day at school we sit with each other
Y ou are the luckiest person in the world when you have
   a best friend like mine.

Bobby Scott (6)

Brill Brother

Sweet, gentle, caring and kind,
My brother is the best person you can find.
He is always happy, he's just one big smile
And, of course, he's got style.
Playing on his bike is his favourite thing
And my nickname for him is The King!
He is only three years old
And even now he is as good as gold.
Making me laugh every minute of the day,
He always asks me to come out and play
In the garden, standing there
In all that beautiful summer air.
Sometimes he shouts but not for long,
And when he's done, he sticks out his tongue.
Sweets and chocolate are his favourite foods,
And to be honest, he really is a cool dude!
If I'm upset, he makes me feel better
By putting on his silly sweater.
He means the world to me
And that's what I want him to see.
Playing with Mitchell, his best friend,
My brother, Toby, likes his friends.
He helps me every day,
And that's all that's left to say.

Chloe Oliver (11)

My Magnificent, Marvellous, Magical Mum

My magnificent, marvellous, magical mum,
Magnificent as she is,
Mum will always push through,
Although she has MS.
My mum will help me
When I fall or cry, she'll be there.
My mum, she's the best!

Chloe Quayle (10)

Mikah's Favourite Bunch

I don't have a favourite person,
I have favourite people instead,
They all mean as much to me
As getting enough rest for school in bed.

My friend Laurie, in Turkey we met,
She came to my nanny's and we looked at holiday pics on the net.
My two friends at school,
Harley and Olivier, I am always playing with them
Because they are really cool.
But . . .
When I'm at home, my favourite people are Nanny, Daddy . . .
Actually I could mention them all.
I think my auntie is really great,
She's having a baby and I can't wait.
My mommy makes me tidy my room
And when she shouts it sounds like a boom.
With my dad I have so much fun,
Running and playing in the sun.

So once more I will repeat,
Many have a favourite person,
I don't, I have favourite people instead
Who all mean as much to me
As getting enough rest for school in bed.

Mikah Knight (5)

Lemonade Jade!

My favourite person is Jade.
She likes lemonade,
She likes being joked,
But doesn't like getting soaked.
She is very kind,
She helps me, I find.
My favourite person is Jade.

Hannah Gordon (8)

27

The Bliss Of My Sis . . .

(This poem is dedicated to my sister, who has done so much for me and taught me that you can succeed at anything if you try)

Some say sisters are annoying,
Some say they're just plain mean!
Well I totally disagree with that -
'Cause mine is like a queen!

I bet yours doesn't like games or fun,
Or make an *excellent* cup of tea.
Well, listen with both ears, folks,
My sister is *all* of those three!

My sister is a doctor and dude,
She's serious but loves to *par-ty!*
I can tell you a thing or two, my friend,
My sis is as cool as can be.

She's there as a shoulder to lean on,
Or to play with, or do fun things!
She's a great role model, and she always reminds me
That to be cool, you don't always need bling!

So now you've got the idea
Of what life is like with my sis and me.
She's a great sister, as you've seen,
The greatest there ever can be!

Rojah Thayabaran (10)

I Just Can't Decide

My favourite person
I just can't decide
So many to choose from
Favourite people where do they come from?
Mum, Dad, brothers too
The rest just too many
What do I do?

Owen Orchard (9)

G Is For Giorgio

I own a cat named Giorgio
Did I mention he's black?
He's the best wherever he goes
And he never does slack
In the morning he wakes
A big yawn to start his day
Leaps off the sofa to give a big shake
And doesn't care if the sky is grey
His back stands upright
To mark his joy
Soon day turns to night
When he plays with his toy
He is a boy who is so gentle and sweet
Oops! But when he spots a bird . . .
They squeak, *tweet, tweet,*
A little song I pretend I had not heard . . .
One of the reasons he is so special to me
Is because Giorgio trusts me *big time!*
And I like that responsibility
I wouldn't swap it for any amount of dimes
However, it doesn't matter if Giorgio is thin or fat
Because he's my cat
And I love him!

Chloe Verebelyi (10)

My Dad Is The Best

My dad is the best,
I put him to the test.
He is funny and cool
And really quite tall.

My dad chases and tickles,
We get in lots of pickles,
We laugh all the time.
My dad's all mine!

Thomas Browne (8)

Who Is It?

She helps me when I need her
At times I need her most
She cooks me most of my meals
I especially like toast

Who is it?

Her cuddles are warm and friendly
She gives me them a lot
She's been there all my life
Even when I was in a cot

Who is it?

She helps me with my homework
Even the toughest stuff
She'll always be there to protect me
Even when things get really rough

Who is it?

Whether I'm happy or healthy
Or have an upset tum
I know she'll always be there
Who is it?

My mum.

Anna Dovey (9)

Grandad

G randad is my strongest strength
R especting him is what I do the best
A lways encouraging me
N ever saying no to get anything I want
D eveloping me and my thoughts
A dvising me for the best
D oesn't stop me fulfilling my desires!

He lives far from me, but is close to my heart!

Ruhi Shah (10)

My Mother

My favourite person is my mother,
I could never wish for another.
She has been with me since I was born,
My love for her can never be torn.
She is the best mum there could ever be,
And is perfect just for me.
I love her in many ways,
My feelings for her grow throughout the days.
They glisten and shine like the stars,
I'm sure they can be seen all the way to Mars.
She has done so much for me,
She's just fab, isn't she?
To make me happy, she is so keen,
In my opinion she should be queen.
And every time I'm in fright,
She cheers me up with all her might.
And I have made a final decision,
To make her happy, that's my mission.
And until this world comes to an end,
She will be my forever friend.
I want her to know I love her a lot,
And that there will always be a place for her in my heart.

Fahimah Dalla (11)

My Sister Is The Best

I love my sister,
I am glad she is not a mister,
She's the best,
Out of all the rest.

My sister doesn't shout,
And she always, always helps me out.
She lets me get her up in the morning,
When she's still tired and yawning.
My sister is the best!

Catriona Baker (10)

31

Someone Special

My favourite person in the world,
I've known them from day one.
It's someone very close to me,
But not my Uncle Ron.

It's not that I don't like him,
In fact he's rather nice.
It's just that on my birthday,
He got me seven mice.

No, she's really much more special,
In fact she's solid gold,
Because when she was created,
They definitely broke the mould.

The years of care and love she's given,
The endless months of work,
She's done it gladly every day
And never received a perk.

It's not my gran or Santa Claus,
Not even my little brother,
My favourite person in the world
Of course, it is my mother.

Kya Robinson (10)

Me And My Dog

My dog Chas makes me smile and is my best friend.

He is my partner in fighting the forces of evil
Even though it's just pretend.

His whiskers tickle me and make me laugh.

He is so big and brave
Until it's time for a bath.

He cheers me when I'm sad and is loyal and true.
I hope you have someone like him in your life too.

Reece Cunningham (6)

My Favourite Person

She is humorous and enthusiastic,
Amiable and quite fantastic,
Though sometimes she does get tired of me,
But then I really still like her you see.

We call her Coco but that's not her name,
We've called her that since she came,
I've known her since Year 4,
And the first time she came she laughed at the door!

She calls me a funny person too,
But I don't think that is true,
She lives in a house near to ours,
Funnily enough we have the same cars.

She has many very good talents,
Especially sports and gym with her balance,
We always play tennis together,
But she beats me in any old weather!

Lastly, I really do think she's fantastic,
I also still think she's enthusiastic,
She's the very best, best friend to me . . .
And her name is Eleni!

Charlotte Hamilton (10)

My Friend Jessica

Jessica is my best friend
And we play with each other a lot
We will play with each other right to the very end
We like to scheme and we like to plot

Summer days spent playing and skipping
Winter days spent building and sledging
We spend days together at school and at play
Best friends forever!
We will always stay!

Emily Booth-Rodgers (9)

My Dog . . . The Love We Share

She has a golden tail,
A fluffy coat,
And a perfect diamond, formed on the centre of her head.
Her paws are oversized, but soft as a silk,
As she pads along the ground.

But then she sees it,
Whizzing around in the sky,
Striped yellow and black,
It buzzes,
She cocks her head to one side,
Whimpers, and pounces!

Trapped under her paw,
It buzzes feebly,
She huffs, and sags into a heap.

You laugh at her relief,
It's finally been caught.

Then you realise,
Your heart has melted,
And you think,
I love you Taz!

Rebecca Prodger (11)

My Favourite Person

My favourite person is
Loyal, kind, friendly and funny.

My favourite person is
Beautiful, intelligent and generous.

My favourite person is
Thoughtful, caring and grateful.

My favourite person is all she can ever be . . .
My best friend.

Jessica McClintock (10)

Podger

My favourite person isn't a cat or a dog
My favourite person isn't a rabbit or a frog
My favourite person likes chocolate and cheese
My favourite person isn't hard to please

My favourite person isn't my dad or my mum
My favourite person has a bit of a tum
My favourite person likes playing with his ball
My favourite person comes when you call

My favourite person isn't a person at all
My favourite person isn't very tall
My favourite person runs about very fast
My favourite person would never come last

My favourite person is furry like mice
My favourite person is cute and nice
My favourite person hasn't got a tail
My favourite person doesn't even wail

My favourite person is a hamster, you see
My favourite person is also 3
My favourite person likes snuggling in his bed
My favourite person likes being fed.

Gemma Anderson (11)

My Guardian Angel

He wakes me at night when I have a nightmare
I call out for him
Uncle David, my guardian angel
Please come
He keeps me happy
He tells me to not litter but recycle
To keep the planet blue and green
My favourite person is my uncle
Who's yours?

Ellis George (11)

My Mum

When I was younger
I called her Mummy
That was when
She had a big tummy

As I've grown older
I call her Mum
Her tummy has been replaced
With a rather large bum

She's there when I need her
She wipes my tears away
We have lots of fun together
We sing and laugh and play

I don't know what I'd do
Without her by my side
She makes me feel safe
And fills me with pride

So Mum, I'll always love you
And would just like to say
I'm so glad you're mine
Don't ever go away!

Rhianna Collins (10)

My Mum

My mum is very thoughtful and kind
And so smart,
But most of all she has a big heart
And I can tell her anything.
I fit in her heart like a diamond ring.
She's the only mum I'd choose if I could,
I love her so much, I know I should.
It is not hard to describe her,
To be honest, to me she's like a goddess.

Tia Burns (9)

My Mom

My mom's one in a million, I'm sure that you would agree,
If you don't believe me then come and take a walk with me,
She's wonderful, she's amazing, my truly fantastic mom,
Upon these pages I now write of all the things she's done.

Well she cleans and cooks and makes the bed,
She laughs and plays and has always said,
'Un-knit your eyebrows or you'll knit a jumper!'
'Be kind to your sister it's not nice to thump her!'

She texts, she hugs, she kisses and jokes,
She loves to have long hot soaks,
We chat, we cuddle, we have a little snuggle,
And she loves to have a cup of tea made by me!

She is my best friend and we have a big trend,
And I can always share my troubles and fears,
But the best thing about her because I couldn't live without her,
Is that she always dries my tears.

Now we're nearly at the end,
But I haven't told you the best bit friend,
She's one in a million you see
And that's because she loves *me!*

Emily Crocker (11)

My Special Nanny

(Dedicated to my loving nan)

Every time I see her,
She brightens up my day
And I want everybody
To know I want to say . . .
She blooms each and every day,
But especially in May.
I love her today
And every day.

Jessica Hawkins (10)

Ambi And Me

Ambi and me,
He's such an adventurous guinea,
That whenever we're together there's something to do,
Always something to do for Ambi and me.

He scratches and squeaks,
But I still know for sure,
He's comfy and happy,
'Cause he smiles at me as I stroke his paw.

He is so cute and cuddly,
He always beams when he sees me,
He is my very best friend,
My very best friend is he.

When he wants to rest,
But not for me to go away,
He just sits in his bedroom,
And lets me feed him hay.

When I call him cheekyminks,
I'm very certain that he winks,
It's always us two,
Ambi and me.

Danni Rees (9)

My Favourite Person Is My Mum

My favourite person is my mum,
She has an incredibly large bum.
She dances and sings
And wears lots of bling
And still thinks she's a young thing.
Her heart is made of gold
And when she is old,
She will still make us laugh with her crazy ways
And we'll remember our growing up days.

Katie Phillips (11)

My Lovely Little Brother, Tom

I used to be a lonely boy
And not have many friends
But I didn't know that it wouldn't be long
Before the arrival of my lovely little brother, Tom

On that bright October morn my mum felt ill
So they rushed her off to hospital
And on that day there came along
My lovely little brother, Tom

Well Tom and I, we got along
Going on adventures from America to Hong Kong
Without ever leaving our back garden
Me and my lovely little brother, Tom

Tom and I are the best of friends
After falling out we'll make our amends
Camp out at night in our little tent
Life would be just a dream

We've grown a lot from being 5 and 7
From being little boys - we're now 9 and 11
How we've grown, my oh my
My lovely little brother Tom and I.

George Starkie (11)

My Favourite Person

My favourite person is my nan
Let me tell you she is so grand
She makes my day when I come to stay
She cooks me chicken and rice
It makes my tummy feel nice
We talk and laugh, we have fun and games
My nan's the best, this is what I say
That's why I like to stay with her
On my holidays.

Naomi Nwagwu (8)

39

My Pets

My kitten is Kiwi,
he likes me,
my kitten is lovely,
he's very cuddly.

My chicken is cheeky,
she pecks peas,
I like Rusteeze,
she cuddles me.

My cat is Stinkee,
she rubs around my knee,
she's very, very old,
she's in our family.

Kimmy is my hen,
she's brown and feathery,
she comes when she is called
to say hello to me.

Shimmer is my brother's pet
who comes inside to try to peck,
a hen so brave, a hen so bold,
she does not do what she is told!

Cherisse Joy Wiggins-Browne (7)

My Dad

My dad is my favourite person because
He does delicious cooking every day.
He takes me to my horse every day,
He is a hard worker.
He gives me wonderful cuddles,
He looks after our family.
He has a good sense of humour,
He always has time for me.
My dad is just simply the best!

Lucy Kent (10)

The Missing Idol!

I have no favourite person
Because I love them all
But all for different reasons
They're there to catch me when I fall

My mum is always there
To comfort and to care
And when I'm sad or down
She turns that frown around

My sister is dreadfully silly
My sister is a pest
But I can't stay without her
Because she is the best

There are no better moments
Than when I'm with my dad
Because we play and laugh
When he is near I am glad

Now that you can see
There are lots of favourites for me
But the reasons aren't the same
Neither are the names.

Gledisa Musollari (11)

Together

My favourite person will make me smile
Even when the day is grey.
When I'm angry she will calm me down.
We get on well and have a laugh,
She raised me and so I love her with all my heart,
And always will.
My favourite person is my mum,
She is always there for me
And I will always be there for her.

Amelia Wise (11)

My Favourite Person

I love my little puppy dog
His name is Patchy Woo
I love my brother, Niall
Whose favourite colour's blue

I love my sister, Niamh
Who has lovely, long brown hair
But my favourite person in the world
Is Mr Markey with grey hair

He was funny and taught me well
He made me good at art
He taught me loads and was the best
He made me really smart

He joked about, we had good fun
He let us play out in the sun
He could bake biscuits and brown bread
He made us lovely buns

In June I had to leave behind
My favourite teacher ever
He was fun and helped me out
He'll be my friend forever

Roisin Cranney (10)

Untitled

My favourite person
Is my mum,
She's loving, kind and full of fun.
I love her more than you will know,
Because she has such love to show.
She picks me up when I am down,
And makes me smile and never frown.
I'd run a mile to be with her,
No one else can be as favourite as she is.

Jordan Fripp (9)

My Special Friend

I have a friend,
He can bend.
His name is Umair,
Sometimes I call him a pear.

He had a pet,
But he gave it to the vet.
We went on a trip
And saw some ships.

We ate chips
With our lips,
We had a pain,
It stopped and came again.

We went to Spain
And we saw a lion with a mane.
We both went to Mars
To get some stars.

We went to Rome
To eat a bone.
At last we went home,
But we still talked on the phone.

Mohammad Naseh Omar (10)

My Loving Mum

She inspires me every day
In a new but lovely way.
She helps my tears fade away
With her special magic touch that day.
When I struggle she's always there,
Even with time to spare.
My love for her is non-stop,
For my heart holds everlasting love.
My loving mum.

Olivia Bruce (11)

My Grandmother

I close my eyes,
She is there in her armchair,
Arms wide open
Ready to embrace me.

My mind wanders,
A smile appears on her wrinkled face.
I run towards her,
I smell her sweet perfume,
She leans forward to kiss me.

I dive deeper into my imagination,
She bounces me gently on her knee.
My eyes twinkle,
I am enchanted by her stories.

I sink into my memories,
I smile in a funny way.
She chuckles softly,
I too am laughing soon.

I open my eyes,
She is no longer there.
I am now alone.

Lucy Summerfield (10)

My Brother

My brother's name is George
he has a broken arm
he did that playing football
and caused us all alarm!
But even though he's clumsy
or getting in my way
and also when we're fighting
I just want to say . . .
I love you George!

Caitlin Chatfield (11)

Iona

She's so fantastic,
She's really, really great,
She's called Iona
And she's my bezzie mate.

What a great friend,
She is to me,
She'll be my friend forever,
Most definitely.

When I'm sad,
She makes me happy,
Even though
I can be a bit yappy.

I can't believe it,
We've never fallen out,
She won't be mean to me
And she'll never ever shout.

She's so fantastic,
She's really, really great,
She's called Iona
And she's my bezzie mate!

Kimberley Oshinowo (11)

My Dad!

My dad, he does a lot of cool things,
But I hate it when he sings!
When he is in very bad cheer,
He can be cheered up by a beer!
Me and Dad sit on the couch,
Me and Dad wince and say 'Ouch!'
For we are watching the TV show 'Crash',
Whilst Mum is making bangers and mash!
My dad loves me and I love him!

Jack Hardiman (9)

My Cat, Fluffy

Fluffy is like my sister,
Even though she is 14.
In cat years that is 72
And she is not even bigger than me!

I just wish she was a human
Then she could talk to me,
That would be so great,
But she might drink my mum's tea!

I have known Fluffy since I was born,
She eats my leftovers too,
But I know that she cares for us,
So we care for her too.

When I sit next to her
She headbutts my knee,
And when it is a sunny day,
She climbs up the tree!

I wish I was an only child
So it was just her and me,
And when I go on the trampoline,
She comes on with me.

Bethany Wattam (10)

My Favourite People

My favourite people are Nana and Grandad,
They are oh so special to me.
They make me happy when I'm sad,
We are so lucky to have them around.
My nana and grandad are so, so sweet,
Shopping for us all, what a treat!
They give up their time for us,
They love us and we love them.
Where would we be without them?

Francesca Lewis (11)

My Favourite Person 2009

My favourite person is my mum,
Mostly because she's loads of fun.

My favourite person is my dad,
Probably because he rarely gets mad.

My favourite person is my sis,
'Cause when I'm out, it's me she'll miss.

My favourite person is my nan
Because she is a fan.

My favourite person is my grandad
Because he is never, ever bad.

Aunts and uncles,
Nans and grans,
Brothers and sisters,
Mums and dads . . .

How hard it is to decide
My favourite person 2009,
So up for nomination I have put
My whole family,
Each and every one!

Megan Whitehouse (11)

Who Am I?

She is on TV
She might have a CV
She is in care
But they all don't share

She is always loud
And entertains a crowd
She is always very bold
But really she has a heart of gold

Who is she?

Courtney Doughty (11)

47

Miss Russell

Miss Russell, my primary school teacher,
Was a truly inspirational preacher.
She would brighten up our day
With what she would say
And lead us to our future.

Miss Russell oozed loads of style,
Mostly because of her perfect smile,
With her long brown hair
And fashion flare,
A quality that is so very rare.

It was strange to me
To see her a bride to be,
Getting married to Trevor with a capital T.
She will always be
Miss Russell to me.

She would teach us without a fear
And she was always so very clear.
The description that she would provide
Made us feel good deep down inside,
And when we all left Year 6 we cried.

Olivia Boutwood (11)

My Dedicated Dance Teacher

Miss Laura is my lovely, graceful dance teacher
I can't wait, don't want to be late
After school we drive the miles, to see her smiles
What shoes to choose, ballet, tap or jazz?
With her kind and patient style
I will learn it in a while
Nutcracker, Coppelia, Swan Lake and Sleeping Beauty, I love them all
The tutus are so pretty, but the sequins are so small
She always makes things fun
Even when she tells me to squeeze my bum!

Annabel Jane Bald (10)

My Best Friend Jack

My best friend Jack is a dog
His fur is golden-brown,
his tongue is pink with black spots
and his nose is black and moist.

He loves to suck his teddy and
chew his bone,
but most of all
he likes to roam.

When I mention walk
his ears go up and down,
but when he is so excited
he looks all around.

When I go to school
Jack lays on the floor,
but always waiting
by the front door.
but when I come home
he lays on his back,
I then give him a cuddle
because he is my best friend Jack.

Claire Thorne (10)

My Favourite Person Is My Mum

My favourite person is my mum,
She really likes to hum.
My mum is kind and understanding,
But she can be quite demanding.
She used to collect pretty rocks,
But now she likes to play the Xbox.
She used to collect us from school
And then take us to the pool.
I love my mum, she is the best,
Way better than all the rest.

Emma Grant (11)

My Favourite Person

My brother is always there for me
No matter what I do
He cares for me in a way
That is unbelievably true.
I looked up to him when I was little
And I still do now
I am his little sister
And that makes me so proud.
We do argue a lot
But what brother and sister won't?
My mum is always there
To stop us and have a moan.
But I wouldn't have it any other way
I love my mum and my brother
They're the best family in the world!
And I wouldn't want another.
I would never admit to him
That he is my favourite person
I love him to the very end
He's not just my big brother
He's also my best friend.

Cheyeanne Nicholas (11)

Miss Bryson

My favourite person is my teacher,
She is always there,
Without a care,
Leaving her knowledge with others.

Miss Bryson is her name,
And this will give her fame,
If it's published in a book,
I want everyone to know,
So come on give me a go,
And let everyone else take a look.

Jack Crockwell (11)

My Dog, Tigger!

He may not be the smartest,
He may not be complete,
But when he is next to me
He always likes to eat!
He always stays with his bro,
They never do depart,
But if they lie down long enough
They really look like hearts.
He lies down with me when he's tired
But when he rolls over he looks like wire.
He does some backwards sneezing
When he's glum and sad
But Mum says he's pretending
And it makes her really mad!
He puts his ears inside out
When he wants some air,
But really he's so fluffy
All you can see is hair!
This has to be the end of my poem,
But Tigger's the best
And you know I'll show them.

Dionne Holmans-Price (9)

My Dad

This poem is about my dad,
He moans at me when I'm mad,
He thinks I'm a monkey,
Because I'm so funky,
And he never thinks that I'm bad.

Because my dad's name is Mark,
He is always up for a lark.
My dad plays ball,
I think he's a fool,
And that is about my dad.

Charlie Harris (9)

51

My Nannan

My nannan is so kind to me,
she lets me stay for tea,
she's the prettiest woman on Earth,
if you saw her you would see.

She lets me go to work with her,
and even restock the shelves,
if she's too busy hugging me then they can
serve themselves.

Every day I want to see her,
and hug her until I drop,
at work she lets me have more than
just a lollipop.

Her name is Shirley,
her hair was curly,
I used to call her curly Shirley.

Now I'm out of breath,
it's time to stop the rhyming,
it took 30 seconds,
now that's perfect timing.

Jade Fogg (10)

My Best Friend

My friend, Fabien, is so cool
We love to go swimming in the local pool
We play football together
We're both in the local team
And when we win we will scream
'Hooray, hooray, hooray.'

We play on his trampoline
Or he comes round mine
A true friend
Come rain or shine.

Matthew Feetenby (10)

Leila

She always makes me smile
And when she's there she always
Makes everything worthwhile.

If you're feeling down she's sure to be a clown.
She's a girl who's very potty and she's never, ever naughty.
This person is good luck
Although she never gets covered in muck.

Her favourite colour's blue
And she knows a lot of facts, like pandas eat bamboo,
Or that birds don't actually go *coo-coo*.

I love her because she's not perfect,
But she doesn't have many flaws.
But don't get on her bad side
Or else you'll hear so many *roars!*

Her qualities never end, like her kind and helpful nature,
Although we tend to bicker, she's the best
And definitely better than the rest.
Yes, you guessed who my favourite person is . . .
It's my 13-year-old sister, Leila.

Madiha Chuimi (10)

Jasper

My favourite person is my brother Jasper,
I love him more than bowls of pasta,
we both like a tickled tummy and
jumping up and down on Mummy,
we both like flying our kites and
playing danger on our bikes.

Sometimes he makes me sad,
but mostly he makes me glad,
that he's my baby brother,
and for that I'd never want another.

Georgia Light (8)

My Mr Edd

Mr Edd is the pony I ride.
I needed someone to help me decide
If I should start riding again
With Amy, my very special friend.

Then one Friday I saw her ride
And then that helped me to decide,
So I booked a lesson for the following Sunday
And was bursting to tell everyone at school on the Monday.

I was only a learner at the start
And now I give it all my heart.
I needed a leader and a very big kick,
But then I just got the nick.

And now I have the time of my life
Cantering through a field with all my might.
Life was never the same
Till I started riding again.

And that is why I wrote this poem about Edd
And I'm sure he'd be happy with everything I've said.
Mr Edd is definitely the one that makes me smile.

Olivia Matano (12)

My Best Friend!

O liver Maiden, Oliver Maiden,
L ovely as a friend,
I will vote a 10, 10, 10,
V oting is hard for a friend but I'll still give him a 10,
E very day I look forward to meeting him,
' R ight, right, right,' says Miss Collins as he gets all the questions right!

Oliver Maiden, Oliver Maiden,
Lovely as a friend.
He will be my friend
Until the very end.

Joshua Jones (9)

My Grandad

My grandad is so funny,
He'll be silly all the time,
Whenever he thinks of something,
He'll always sing a rhyme.
Although his hair is silver,
He always thinks it's blond,
Of keeping food in his tache,
He is very fond.
Christmas is a special time
When he comes to stay with me,
Sneaks with the presents wiggling under the tree.
He's very good at cards,
One for a jack, crib and more,
He also does his weird stories
That make my laughter sore.
I went on holiday with him
To a place near Ripon,
When he walked on the beach,
He had trousers and a woolly jumper on . . .
But I still love him!

Emily Crick (10)

My Mother

My mother is young, intelligent, loving and caring and a mother who never
gives up.
When you need a favour doing it's done as fast as a cheetah.
When something is cleaned by her there's not a speck of dust.
When something needs doing it's done right away.
My mother is a marvellous mother, a mother who I love.
When my mother makes some food, it smells like a small bunch of red roses.
When my mother irons my clothes there's not a single crease.
My mother is young, intelligent, loving and caring and a mother who never
gives up.

My mother is a dream come true.

Amina Bibi (11)

Mummy, Mummy

My mummy is my loving person,
Happy, happy, happy, happy.
My mummy is a teacher,
Jolly, jolly, jolly, jolly.
My mummy is a baker,
Curly wurly, curly wurly.
My mummy is a singer,
Fantastic, fantastic.
My mummy is a cooker,
Yummy, yummy, yummy, yummy.
My mummy is a doctor,
Healthy, healthy.
My mummy is a superstar,
Goodie, goodie, goodie, goodie.
My mummy is a collector,
Hooray, hooray.
My mummy is a carer,
Pleasantly please
And now we know she's the
Best mummy ever!

Methusa Nikethan (8)

My Dog

My dream day came,
travelling to the dog's home again.
We looked in every cage that came our way,
but we couldn't see what we wanted on this dream day.
As I turned sadly to go home,
I saw this dog all alone.
I knew she was the one for me,
so did all my family.
We were thinking of a name for you,
all of us came up with Bonny Blue.

I love you Bonny Blue!

Tanya Rose Hanlon (9)

My Favourite Person Is My Grandad

My grandad has silvery grey hair
With wrinkles all over his face
Which look like train tracks.
My grandad also has sparkly green eyes.
My grandad sometimes tells stories,
Sometimes I understand, sometimes I don't.
But most of all, I know my grandad
Will always care for me and love me.
My grandad buys me sweets,
Some I like, some I don't,
But it was the thought that counts.
When it's my birthday,
He sometimes gets me presents I need
And presents I don't need.
When my grandad gets his photo album out
And shows me pictures of him,
He always describes them so well.
I want to hear the stories again and again,
But most of all, I love my grandad
And he loves me.

Georgina Gachette (9)

Jagoda Lipka

J agoda is an excellent friend
A friend who makes me laugh
G rateful for everything I give her
'O h my God,' she says when I give her a Scooby
D elightful friend she is
A nd she is absolutely helpful

L ovely handwriting and drawing
I think Jagoda will be an artist
P eople like Jagoda because she's funny
K eisha is her friend too
A lot of friends Jagoda has got.

Latesha Durham (9)

My Favourite Person

My favourite person
Of the year,
Is the one
Who's always near.
Near in age,
Near in looks,
Near in a love
Of reading books.
He teases me
To make me tough,
But protects me
If things get rough.
And although
We're always fighting,
We go together
Like thunder and lightning.
This special person
Is like no other,
My favourite person
Is my brother!

Rachel Coombes (13)

My Grandma

My favourite person is my . . . grandma!

She lives in Bangladesh,
her house smells so fresh,
she gives me anything,
it's like she has a magic ring,
she gives me yummy food,
and she is never, never rude.

That's my favourite person,

My grandma,
(There's no one like my grandma!)

Sharmina Maisha Rashid (9)

My Favourite Person

My first favourite person is my mum,
She's always just a big ball of fun,
She's never down and never glum,
That's why I like my mum.

My second fave person is my dad,
He really is not that bad,
If he's cross he rarely gets mad,
That's why I like my dad.

My third favourite person is my nan,
I love her that much, I'm her number one fan,
As for a joke, I always say, 'Yeah, man,'
That's why I really like my nan.

My fourth favourite person is my auntie,
Her fashion sense is really fancy,
When we have a party, she gets really dancey,
That's why I really, really like my auntie.

I'll stop right here or else I'll write about all my family,
We all may be different but we all live in perfect harmony.

Mahira Zahoor (11)

My Favourite Person

My favourite person is called Miley,
She's 15 years old and she's really smiley.

She stars as Hannah in a really big show
And paparazzi follow her everywhere she goes.

I bite my nails the same as her
And she loves cute puppies with lots of fur.

Cheerleading is her favourite sport,
She loves to dance around the baseball court.

Miley is smart, funny and cute,
And if there's a new shop, she's there in a shoot!

Bethany Brown (10)

59

My Favourite Person

My favourite person in my life is my two year old brother Rio.
Rio is the best, better than the rest
Rio is the best, out of all the rest.

Rio is my brother, we get up to a lot, our mam always loses the plot.

I have enjoyed many things, but the best of all was when he came.

When I go to school, he has no one to play with,
but he will always know that he is my favourite.

He is what I wake up for every morning,
he always brings a smile on his way to play.

I respect him so much but you can't forget
our mam and dad, they give us so much.

I have carried a lot of memories before and after he came,
they will always stay with me in my heart and brain.

Rio is the best, better than the rest,
Rio is the best out of all the rest.

I love you loads Rio!

Imarni Old (11)

Miley Cyrus

I think Miley
Is so great,
I'd give her
A 5-star rate.
She has two sisters
And two brothers,
She also lives
With a father and mother.
She was bullied
At her school,
But I think
She's very cool.

Rebecca Austwick (10)

A Person Is A Person

A person is a person
But when it comes to it,
This person is special.
He doesn't have to be close,
He doesn't have to be near,
But when he is close,
The warmth in your heart
Certainly isn't fear.

You don't have to ask,
You don't have to say a word,
Because when you're loved,
Everything can be heard.

He will be known through history
For sharing and caring for you and me
And we all know it will be known
And we all know it will be shown

And that's why this person
Is my favourite person.

Reagan Collins (11)

My Favourite Person

I say, I say, who do I talk to all day?
A friend,
A pal,
A special person,
My favourite person is Morgan,
She is so wonderful and special,
When I lose in games, she is so kind
To make me feel better.
When you have a favourite person,
Keep them or you will never succeed.
Enjoy what you have with them,
Feel better.

Nana Bonsu (11)

My Friend Uncle John

John is my uncle
He's a bit like a friend
He's really very funny but drives my
Grandma round the bend.

John has a trick he does specially for us
He takes a pea with his tongue and puts it up his nose
And we wonder and wonder where it all goes!

A few minutes later his tongue pops out
The pea is on the end and we all give a shout!

He's actually 44 but very immature
He puts silly things on his head including our hamster's bed.

But we love it when he comes to stay
As we have lots of favourite games to play
From Charades to Uno or even a lesson in Bingo
John always behaves like a bit of a dingo!

So hip hip hooray for John, my very nutty uncle
Without him in my life, it wouldn't be much funcle!

Georgia Cox Lousada (9)

My Favourite Person

My favourite person is my brother,
Because we play loads of games
And chase each other.

He makes me laugh when he eats his tea,
But I laugh even more
When he tickles me.

He snores all night but sings all day
And he asks for me when I'm away.

I love my brother but he can be a pain,
I love him to bits
Come sunshine or rain.

Bryony Twinney-Roche (9)

Mum!

She reads to me every day,
I love it when she stops to play.
Who is it?
Mum!
And when she has to do the dishes,
I'd like to give three big kisses
For
Mum!
But when the day is nearly over,
I find a four-leaf clover
For Mum!
Now it's nearly time for bed,
She puts the covers up to my head,
Who is it?
Mum!
My mum helps me with lots of things,
I just wish I had some wings
To help
Mum!

Georgina Dare (9)

Mom Is The Word

Mother who bore me, mother who gave me
The material that constructed who I am today,
Showering me with immense love and mercy
I can't repay.
Enduring sleeping through storms of tears
To attend to me, her dear.

She gave me wings to be free,
She granted me sense to be me.
I can see her halo, she is my saving grace.
She is everything I need and more.
It's written all over her face.
She is my hero, my angel, my saving grace.

Lesley-Ashley Nganje (12)

This Person And I

There is one special person in my life, who no one can match.
We are very attached, this person and I.
This person loves me through and through and gives me ideas
when I haven't a clue.
We talk, we walk, we love, we laugh, this person and I.
I can tell this person my worries and fears.
She will not giggle or sneer, just listen, just listen.
We are the best of friends, this person and I.
This person makes sure that I have fun.
Even when the jobs are not done.
We are close and inseparable, this person and I.
I would be lost if this person wasn't here.
This person helps me through the things that I doubt
And they always turn out alright in the end.
I love this person, my favourite person.
There is one special person in my life, who no one can match.
This person and I.
I and this person.
Me and my mum.

Ellie Loxton (11)

My Favourite People

My mum is nice:
I like it when we go girlie shopping
She makes me laugh
I like it when she tucks me into bed
My favourite thing about my mum is she cares about me
I love her because she is a wonderful mum.

My dad is nice:
I like it when we go swimming
He makes me laugh
I like it when he tickles me
My favourite thing about my dad is he cares about me
I love him because he is a wonderful dad.

Leia Riddell (9)

My Brilliant Dad!

My favourite person,
Who could it be?
One of my idols,
That's easy for me.
My dad, of course,
He is the one,
Whether I'm upset
Or having fun.
He'll make me happy,
Sun or rain,
On a boat
Or on a plane,
On our bikes
Or over the park,
We're early to bed
But up with the lark.
I always want to make him proud
By standing up and shouting out loud
I love you Dad!

Courtney Smith (10)

My Friend

I have a friend,
And Lydia's her name,
She's funny and lively,
But no one's quite the same.
Everyone's unique,
In their own special way,
Lydia's always happy,
And makes me smile every day.
She has a creative mind,
Her writing's straight and neat,
She's arty and adventurous,
And surely a pleasure to meet.

Irene Ashworth (10)

Which Is My Favourite?

Out of my mother
And my brother
I don't know who to choose
Out of the dog
And the cat
I don't know which to choose
Out of the horse
And the bird
I don't know which to choose
Which is my favourite?
My mum is the best
My brother is too
The dog is just so cute
The cat chases mice away
And the horse is fun to ride
The bird whistles good . . .
But I choose my mum
Because she cooks and cares for me
And she helps me with nearly everything!

Yasmin Taghvaipour (9)

My Mum

My favourite person is my mother,
She loves me like no other.
She cooks me dinner every day,
Even though I do not pay!
She does my washing all the time
And pegs it out on the line.
She's always there to help me out,
Even though I scream and shout.
She makes me better when I'm ill,
She goes to the doctors to get me a pill.
My favourite person is my mother
Because she loves me like no other.

Rhys Darbyshire (11)

My Favourite Person

My favourite person is Santa Claus
And his little puppy called Paws

All his magnificent reindeer
And the presents that travel far and near

The dark blue sky
The perfect mince meat pie

Down that chimney
That present's won me

A glass of whiskey
Don't scare the cat Frisby

Rudolph's red nose
They all stop and pose

The clock strikes one
His deed is done

Morning has arrived
Santa has survived.

Lynsey Johnson (11)

Shadow The Dog

Shadow is no badow,
He's the perfect dog indeed,
Although he costs a mountain to feed.
But,
He's no mutt,
With legs like an athlete,
Along with walloping great feet,
In fact he's so big,
He takes up two whole van seats!
I love my dog, Shadow,
Shadow is no badow,
He is the perfect dog indeed!

Zoe Jackman (11)

67

My Cool Cousin

I've a very cool cousin
and her name is Emma G
I look a lot like her
and she looks a lot like me

When we are together
we get along just fine
laughing, singing and dancing
she acts like she is 9

I think she's very thoughtful
she shows a lot of care
she's also very pretty
with her blue eyes and brown hair

She's very, very special
she's my bestest friend ever
she helps me with my homework
because she's really, really clever.

When I grow up I want to be like her.

Olivia Cook (10)

My Big Sis, Robyn

If I had a favourite person it would be,
My sister of course, now you'll see.
She's nice, pretty, caring and kind,
She's the best sister ever, that's what I find.
Blonde hair, brown eyes and she's 23,
Her favourite music is R&B.
She smiles for miles every day,
Sometimes she can moan but that's OK.
She makes me laugh and makes me smile,
She'll always go the extra mile.
Now I've told you, can you see,
Why my sister's so special to me?

Codi Sidwell (10)

My Favourite Person

My mum is helping me all the while,
Sometimes I help her sort through the washing pile,
So sometimes I help her, see,
But mostly it's her helping me.

Every time I come home there'll be food on the table,
Sometimes home-cooked,
Sometimes not,
But let's not turn this poem into a fable.

She's kind to me every day of the week,
Even when things are looking quite bleak.
What I'm trying to get across
Is that sometimes, it can be chaos!

Now I'm starting secondary school and my sister's starting uni,
I can't see how she doesn't get driven up the bend, and go completely loony!
I've always thought my mum is great,
She's not just my mum, she's my best mate.

That's why she's my favourite and best person in the universe!

Joseph Charlton (11)

My Fabulous, Furry, Feathery Family

Kiwi is a tabby cat,
He likes to chase the mice and rats,
Stinkee is a tortie cat,
She likes to lay upon our mat,
Mummy is a lovely mum,
She really likes to tickle my tum!
Daddy is a brilliant dad,
He likes to say, 'Come on my lad!'
Cherisse Joy is a fabulous sister,
When she goes out I really miss her,
I must not forget our feathered friends,
Shimmer, Rusteeze, Kimmy, our happy hens!

Christian Wiggins-Browne (10)

My Friend

My friend has deep brown eyes,
This isn't a game of lies!

He hits people who get his website wrong,
He hits them hard with kitchen tongs!

I like him a lot because he is cool,
He's *not* the type for being told off in class!

He and me are best of friends,
Our friendship never ever ends!

He's a furry, furry little thing,
He has got some sort of zing!

He wears a deep coat of red,
He is always sleeping in my bed!

I've given you some clues
About my little friend
It ends in 'kat' you might have guessed!
It's Alexander the meerkat!

Mary-Pia Jeyarasingham (10)

My Special Mum

My mum is so special,
She is my special friend.
She helps me learn
So I can be top of the class.

She helps me do my homework,
I always get things right.
She helps me with the tricky words,
She helps me to try then try again.

Without my mum I would not be
The girl I am right now,
All grown-up and independent.
I love my special mum.

Cassandra Pearson (8)

70

Rose

Rose was my auntie and filled a huge part in my heart,
So this is why I've written this poem.
Rose loved butterflies,
Twinkling in the corner of your eye,
Gliding through the wonderful blue sky.

Pink, purple, blue, green,
All of them we have seen,
Rose was like a butterfly,
She wasn't a boring blue,
She was a bright yellow,
And her heart was as soft as a marshmallow.

Rose was . . .
Loving, caring and kind,
And had an imaginative mind.
She never let anyone put her down,
She loved her comfy dressing gown!

Love you always, Rose!

Abbie Wedgbury (11)

My Very Special Person

My mum is my very special person
Because she's funny and angry.
This is what she looks like:
She has brown hair, sparkling blue eyes,
My mum has lovely red lips.
My very special person is as happy
As a monkey and my favourite teddy,
Chuckles and laughs a lot.
My mum can be scary and spooky
When she hides behind the door
And jumps out and scares me.
And I remember the day
She jumped out and scared me.

Courtney Wadcock (9)

My Mum's The Best Mum, What About You?

My mum knows when I'm nervous,
She knows when I'm upset,
She loves me no matter what,
Even if I break her favourite pot!

My mum's hair is curly,
She curls it every day.
My beautiful mum lets me use her curlers,
And I don't have to pay!

One of my favourite things is to cook,
She always helps me pick the right book.
She gives me advice on all that I do,
She sometimes even jumps when I shout *boo!*

Thank you, Mum, for all that you have done.
My mum makes sure that I have fun.
Thank you, Mum, you have done a lot for me.
My mum's the best mum!
What about you?

Nicola Hodgkiss (12)

My Favourite Person - Charlotte

I remember Charlotte since she sat in her beautiful cot;
Charlotte is just so funny, she bounces up and down just like her pet bunny;
Now we're older and we have grown, Charlotte has her own pony that she
decided to loan;
Sometimes we ride, but sometimes we hide, it all depends on what we decide;
Charlotte wants to be a nurse, she makes movies about blood and guts, she
doesn't even rehearse;
Charlotte is just so funky, she likes to paint her nails bubblegum pink while
dancing like a monkey;
Charlotte is a one of a kind swimmer, she swims down low and shimmers,
She has a real passion for fashion, she shimmers and glimmers;
Charlotte loves cheese and pickle, it makes her shine like a fairy and twinkle;
Charlie and I are best friends, this kind of friendship *never* ends!

Kary Lee (10)

Mum

(In loving dedication to a wonderful mum)

Generous and loving,
Always there for me,
Kind and forgiving,
That's all she'll ever be.

Thoughtful but funny,
Always makes me laugh,
Clever and sunny,
Never rainy, not a chance!

Wise and creative,
She wants the best for me,
Never frustrated,
Not intentionally.

Talkative and charming,
All the men bow at her feet,
Beautiful and alarming,
Watch out, she's coming down the street!

Carina-Alicia Panchal (11)

Untitled

My favourite person is God
'Cause He gave life to me.
He makes it possible for me to start
my day very nicely.
I get up and out with the legs He gave to me,
I go downstairs for breakfast
And use my eyes to see what looks nice and tasty
And good for my tummy.
I use my ear to listen to my breakfast in my bowl.
Can you guess what I'm hearing?
I hear snap, crackle and pop.
I love God for letting me have Rice Krispies today
That are filling me up.

Pariese Paul (9)

Cassey Is My Favourite Pet

I like to take Cassey to the park
For nice long walks in the dark.
She has an annoying bark.

She loves to fool around,
I love to roll around with her in the park,
But it is even better in the dark.

She likes to chase the ducks,
But that's pushing her luck.

I like to cuddle her when it is rainy outside,
She's so cuddly and warm,
She keeps me safe inside.

I like to play football and to throw her ball
For her when we are outside playing around,
For she just comes bounding around.

But most of all I love Cassey to bits,
Because she is always there.

Cameron Howarth (7)

Dad Is The Best

D ad, I love you so, so much
A ll the time you make me smile
D efending me all the while

I f I need help you are always there
S howing me how much you care

T eaching me right from wrong
H elp is never far along
E ver grateful for your love

B est dad in the world
E ver ready for anything
S o loving yet so giving
T o you, Dad, I love you so!

Reece Kyle Walker (9)

My Dad

He's one of a kind, my dad, the best,
Likes and plays football,
Takes me to watch my team, Reading,
Good-looking (in his own way),
Loves his friends and family,
Cares for them all,
Loves his work,
Gets his wages every week.
Very intelligent,
Went to Reading University
If I can remember.
Has the same taste in music,
Both like U2, Oasis and Kasabian.
Likes his food as well,
Cooks his homemade lasagne
And his wicked Sunday roast.
And he's especially good at being my dad
And that's why I love him.

Joshua Kitchingham (11)

My Nan

My nan is a piece of my heart,
She is the smile on my face,
That sparkles in my eye.
Whenever I need her
She is always there.
She is the sun in my sky,
She is the stars in my night sky.

My nan is my light in the dark,
My nan is my guardian angel.
If I'm alone I just think of my nan
And I will feel safe.
My nan is my soul.
I love my nan.

Sophie Richards (10)

My Mum

You're sweet and kind like cherry pie
Like candyfloss so delicate
You make me laugh, you don't make my cry
Happiness walks by your side
When you smile the sun shines
You're always on the go
But wherever you go you will be looking fabulous
World peace is your thing
Everyone loves it when you sing
You love to shop until you drop
You really like lollipops
Although you would prefer toffee
With a cup of coffee
When the day is done
You love to sit in the sun
That's kinda hard when you
Live in Huyton
So I guess the sofa will have to do for you, Mum!

Chloe Roper (11)

My Friend Kira

It's hard to explain why Kira is my best friend,
Sometimes I hurt her feelings
But she forgives me in the end.

She's got a kind heart and makes me feel special,
When I tell her jokes, she laughs like a devil.

She's my friend in Year 5,
With short hair and brown eyes.
I like her clips shaped as small butterflies.

She's small enough to carry,
But she carries me instead.
It's hard to explain why I like her so . . .
When I'm older, maybe I'll know.

Hayley Penn (9)

HOM

My favourite person is my grandad, HOM,
I will tell you where I get that from!
It stands for 'Hairy Old Monkey',
Which is funny! I hope you can see.
He's taught me about stars in the sky
And answers me when I ask him why.
He's also told me all about Mars,
I mean the planet, not the chocolate bars!
He's good if you need a chat,
But doesn't talk through 'The Bill', even I know that!
He knows just about everything,
And do you know? He can even sing!
He is really clever and can play chess,
But he doesn't like it when I make a mess.
HOM is cool, fab and funny
And is even better than money!
He is the best grandad you could ever meet!
So to put it simply, he is neat!

Haydn Hopkinson (8)

My Brother!

Brothers can be silly at times,
My brother Marcus is that,
By the way he is 10 years old,
But I love him.

When I am hurt he looks after me,
He always takes care of me,
When I am poorly he looks after me.

When he is poorly I look after him,
When he is hurt I look after him,
He can be playful and silly,

But he is still my brother,
I love him as I love myself!

Chernice Angel-Whyte (8)

My Favourite Person Is Santa

Santa is great
I bet he's my mate
He replies to my letter
Which makes me feel better
I met him once in Lapland
I was so excited he shook my hand
He's so very jolly!
He gave me a yummy lolly!
I met his reindeers
They had no fears
They ate lots of hay
Before they pulled Santa's sleigh!
Dasher, Vixen, Comet, Donner and Dancer
Rudolph, Blitzen, Cupid and Prancer
And that was the answer
I knew I wanted to see Santa
On his sleigh
Every single day!

Amy Marland (10)

My Granny

Granny bakes lovely cakes
She is very sweet and always gives us a treat
Granny is really nice
And in her dreams she skates on ice
Swirling and twirling around she goes
Where she stops nobody knows
At the end of the day
She always remembers to give us supper
But also remembers to have her cuppa
Granny is also good at sewing
Now I'm coming to the end of my poem
She really is my super gran
But most of all she's my mother's mam.

Bethany Alisha Thompson (9)

Super Steph

My favourite person is Stephanie,
She's full of life and very bright.
She's very daft and not a height.
She's super cool, that's why she's a silly fool.
Stephanie's fashion sense
Could not be worse,
But when it comes to shopping
She's got no money left in her purse.
Steph loves music,
She will never lose it.
She listens to it every day,
By the end she's got a headache.
She says what she likes
And doesn't care,
But when she's with her mam
She just stands there.
So it's easy to say why
Stephanie is my favourite person!

Emily Carr (10)

My Favourite Person

When I see my sister
I always have an urge to smile,
Whether she's nice or mean,
She treats me like a royal queen.
She buys me lots of toys
Which fills me up with joy,
Though when I'm feeling down,
She turns my frown upside down.
She plays with me a lot
And we make up evil plots.
Our favourite sweets are Jelly Tots.
That's why my sister's the best
Out of all the rest!

Chloe Rosenberg (10)

I Like To Think . . .

I like to think
I'm funny, fun, fantastic.

I like to think . . .
I hope I am . . .

I hope I am
Exciting, eager, enthusiastic.

I hope I am . . .
I like to think . . .

I like to think
I'm marvellous, mega, mostly optimistic.

I like to think . . .
I hope I am . . .

I hope I am
Friendly, fabulous, fair.

I am *my* favourite person!

Madeleine Luszczak (10)

Family

When I got this through my door,
I thought *OMG, no more,*
But then I said this may be hard,
There are so many people I love.
I could write about Mum,
How she is so fun,
Or my dad,
How he can be so bad
(Mainly at singing).
Or my cat, Sarah, fish, Molly,
Dad's dog, Jack, my nans, my grandads,
Auntie, uncle and cousins!
I love them all!

Megan Walder (10)

My Favourite Person

M y favourite person is
Y oung and sweet

F abulous in every way
A lways looking for ways to help
V ery, very helpful each day
O n our own we may fight but always make it
U p
R ight away
I n or out, around the house we
T ry to play
E very second of our life we bond more and more

P laying together is so much fun in
E ach and every way
R ight now you're probably wondering who this person is
S o to your surprise
O f course it's my little sister
N o one loves her as much as I do!

Francesca Taylor (11)

My Favourite Person

My nan is lovely and cuddly,
She makes me laugh until my eyes go runny!
My nan makes the best roast in the world,
She also makes the best jokes in the world!
She's always up for a laugh, my nan,
She'll help with my homework too, if she can!
She lets me stay up late
With many chocolate biscuits on my plate!
My nan is more like a kid, better though,
She'd jump up and down if there was snow!
She lets me sit on her knee.
It's easy to see that I love her
And she loves me too!

Iqra Saged (10)

My Darling Dominic

I have a little brother,
He's really sweet and funny,
Loves to talk and chatter away
To me and my mummy.

He can be cute and charming
When Mummy's doing the ironing,
And wants to buy
Secret Spy.

He really wants a dog,
Which he would call Mog.
They would run around and play
Every day!

You should see his funny faces,
With his cheeky chappy smile,
And laughs for a while!

My darling brother, Dominic.

Sinéad Millar (10)

My Favourite Friend

My favourite person is my friend,
Her name is Ellie
And she likes eating jelly.

Her hair is brown,
Her teeth are white,
She comes to my house every night.

She is always happy as can be
And often enjoys a cup of tea.

She likes a chat about this and that,
She enjoys playing with my cat.

She is my friend as you can see
And she is always, always there for me.

Sophie Ward (8)

82

The Adventures Of My Cousin And I

We've made up lots of dances,
We've made up lots of games,
We've made up lots of silly songs,
With very silly names.

We've had a midnight feast,
We've had a water fight,
We've even had a campfire,
So very late at night.

When we went camping,
We explored the grounds,
We even climbed a high bridge,
That was out of bounds.

So there you have it,
How good times fly,
These are the adventures,
Of my cousin and I!

Arissa Tapper (9)

My Grandma!

My grandma gets stressed out
When me and my sister are messing about.

My grandma doesn't think windmills are serene,
She loves the smell of grass so green.

My grandma likes fish 'n' chips,
Also those ten pence strawberry lips.

My grandma is a cat lover,
She thinks they are no bother.

My grandma loathes football,
She doesn't like it at all.

My grandma thinks flowers are extraordinary,
My grandma loves blackberries.

Jessica Mowthorpe (10)

My Amazing Dad!

My dad's called Richard,
He loves his job.
His boss is called Richard
And they work a lot.

My dad is amazing,
He loves us all to bits.
My dad isn't crazy
And he says we're amazing kids.

Me and my dad love each other,
We really are great friends.
He really loves my mother
And our friendship never ends.

Now I've told you about my father,
I hope you did enjoy
The things that I would rather
Do with lots of joy.

Serena Talbot (10)

Untitled

My cousin, Chloe, is very special to me,
She is always very happy come breakfast, lunch or tea.

Night or day, rain or shine,
She's my favourite person of all time.

We share our secrets when alone,
We're always talking on the phone.

Every minute we can share,
Is very special anywhere.

Up or down, left or right,
We are very close and tight.

If the world could learn by us,
It would be filled with love and trust.

Libby Britnell (9)

Mum

My mum is so amazing,
My mum is the best,
And my mum is so wonderful,
She cares for me a lot,
God bless her forever.

I am always thinking of you,
How can I pay back everything you did?
I just can't because what you have done
For me and my family,
It's just too much!
God bless you forever.

And when I do my homework
She's so helpful.

I can see the world right through her eyes
And that's what makes her
The best mum in the world.

Natalie Enwiya (8)

My Favourite Person

We'll both go shopping for clothes in town,
Jeans, dresses and soft nightgowns.

She'll cook pasta, rice, roasts and more,
She'll wash the dishes and clean the floor.

She does all this without a moan or groan,
Whilst everyone else is chatting on the phone.

Takes me to my school friend's party,
Makes lovely paintings, she's very arty.

Buys chocolates and sweets just for me,
Helps me when I've grazed my knee.

We'll make cakes and desserts just for fun,
My favourite person is my mum!

Maaria Rahman (11)

My Favourite Person

Loves me, looks after me,
Helps me when I'm stuck
And doesn't shout at me
Even when I'm covered in muck.

Driving me to all these places,
No matter if it's early or late.
Yet never expects anything -
Given on a silver plate.

I love my favourite person,
Which is why I'm writing now.
Just to let her know,
That I love her so.

Have I told you who this person is?
I believe that I have not.
So, I'll let you know - it's no bother,
My favourite person is, *my mother!*

Kirsten Friedman (11)

Mum And Dad

Mum plays hard
Dad plays soft.

Mum plays stressed
Dad plays cool.

Mum wears frills
Dad chills.

Mum buys you chocolate
Dad buys you sweets.

Mum buys you clothes
Dad wears vests.

But over all I have to say
They are both equal in every way.

Meghan Jones (10)

My Favourite Person

A star from the heavens,
A daisy in spring,
A smile on my face,
All the joy she brings.

Her straight jet-black hair,
Her heart-warming smile,
The love she provides,
Lasts more than a mile!

Her soft, gentle voice,
Her piercing green eyes,
She loves me to bits,
She'll never tell lies.

So Mummy I love you,
And thanks for it all,
I love how you tell me,
'I'll never let you fall.'

Niamh Connolly (10)

Me And My Dad

Me and my dad go swimming together,
At the Aberdeen Leisure Centre.

Oh, it really is so fun,
When we are out in the sun.

When we are splashing in the water,
The sun is burning, getting hotter.

When we are done we make a deal,
To go to Burger King for a meal.

I say thanks, that was really yummy,
I don't want more, I've got a full tummy.

On the way home I say thanks to my dad,
Today was the best day I've ever had.

Erin-Louise Edmonstone (10)

My Best Friend

My best friend is Robyn,
She smiles all day,
She never stops laughing
When we play.

She always comes round just to say
How are you and have a nice day.
When I am scared she wishes me luck
And tells me not to worry,
Then buys me presents and sends me gifts
In such a great big hurry.

When I am down she comes around
And tells me not to cry.
She cheers me up and gives me a hug
And says, 'Becky, don't be shy.'

My friend, Robyn, she does the lot,
I'm sure she is the nicest friend I've got.

Rebecca Holmes (11)

Mum

No words can begin to describe someone
As beautiful, kind and sweet as my mum.

Her words are magic, she makes you feel good,
Never are you misunderstood.

She's someone to talk to, to tell of your pains,
Whatever they are, you'll feel great again.

To look at her means a smile a day,
She makes you feel happy, carefree and gay.

Her soft ginger hair, her emerald-green eyes,
Reflect how beautiful she is inside.

No words can begin to describe someone
As beautiful, kind and sweet as my mum.

Alexandra Ballard (12)

My Dad Can Do Anything

My dad sleeps
But he still sweeps.
My dad bought me a doll,
He also gave me a dollar.

My dad is so brave,
In this family he is the bravest.
This family is lovely
But my dad is the loveliest.

I can cook
But my dad is the best cook.
I can sing
But my dad is the best singer.

My dad is good at playing the guitar
And my family cannot play the guitar.
My dad can play tennis.
I am bad at it.

Farai Murambatsvina (10)

My Best Friend

My favourite person is my best friend,
She sticks with me until the end.
I met her on the first day of school,
She was really funny, awesome and cool.
The next few years were quite a thrill,
Until she announced on the 5th of April,
'I'm going to move to Ireland,' she said,
I had to sit down and hug my ted.
There are some advantages of her going to Ireland,
I met a lovely girl from Beeston Rylands.
And now I'm coming to the end of my rhyme,
I wish I had more space and time
Because there are lots more things to say.
I hope she will come back one day!

Alicia Berehowskyj (11)

My Mum

I love my mum so very much
Her skin is soft to touch
Her eyes are shiny like pearls
Her hair is long with curls.

My mum is caring and kind
She is a rare type to find
She buys me presents which are great
They are impossible to hate.

My mum taught me how to care
She is beautiful and fair
I will never leave my mum alone
Even when I am fully grown.

My mum is fantastic in every way
She always makes my day
Don't cry in despair
For your mum is out there.

Andrew Abdulahad (11)

Best Mum

My mum is the best
But sometimes I don't let her rest
She is very, very good
But sometimes I spoil her mood.
She was there for me
Even when I was bitten by a bee.
I didn't stop crying
But she kept trying.
She is so sweet
Even more than a sugary treat.
I love my mum
Even though she doesn't let me have gum.
So friends, don't worry about the rest
Because mums are always best!

Juned Malek (8)

Mum

My mum means the world to me
And everything I do
There is nothing that can part us
Because we're stuck together like glue.

You've been the perfect mother
Kind and loving too
I grew strong with your support
Dependable and true.

My mum is always here for me
No matter what I do
She's always there to comfort me
And help me through and through.

Though I may not tell you
I hope you know it's true
You've been a wonderful mother
And I'll always love you.

Kayleigh Clayton (11)

My Favourite Person

My favourite person is someone
Who can read, write and spell.
I like them even though
I don't know them very well.
I like a person who gets
Stuck into a good book.
I also like a person
Who is a very good cook.
I like a person who likes art,
Finishing a painting is like eating a tart.
So my favourite person
Would probably be
Someone who I like
And they like me.

Lily Vie (11)

My Favourite Person

Stepmum, Stepmum,
You're number one.
You laugh and you sing
In front of everyone.

We play lots of games
And read lots of books,
And now you're teaching me
How to cook.

You're silly and funny
And helpful too,
You're as mad as a hatter,
But I'm just like you.

So my favourite person
In the whole world
Has to be my stepmum,
She's better than anyone.

Jessie Annetts (8)

Just One Favourite Person

Just one favourite person is too much to ask,
So I've found a solution to fill the task.
Should it be Mum or should it be Dad?
Leaving one out would make me feel too sad.
My dad plays guitar and really rocks,
He truly is top of the pops.
My mum is as pretty as the world's best model,
And if she entered, she'd win in a doddle.
Dad tells stories with the funniest jokes,
Mum cooks the best eggs with the dippiest yolks.
She cheers me up when I'm feeling down,
Dad makes me smile when I've got a frown.
So I've decided at the end of this poem,
That my favourite person is both of them!

Kai Atkinson (10)

Me And My Bear, Max

Me and Max got into trouble
For eating a Smartie off the chocolate cake
We climbed in my bed
Sang a song to Max's ted
And then got trapped in a bubble

We saw through the glass
My mum drinking out of a flask
As we floated up into the air

Wow, what's that I see?
I think it's a green bumblebee
Max and I blew the bubble closer
What? A frog swinging on that bare brown tree!

If only we hadn't have blown the bubble
We would not have been trapped
Then the rain fell on us
And we both went *splat!*

Deanna Cornell (10)

Jess Is The Best!

Out of all my friends
I picked Jess,
Her room is always a total mess.
She talks of rubber ducks all day,
Maybe even every day!

She loves to be friendly and kind,
She has a bit of a crazy mind.
She can be a bit annoying, I find,
But we still enjoy having a great time.

Jess likes to have a sing-along,
Especially with her favourite song.
I'm sure she'll really adore this rhyme,
If I get it to Young Writers in time!

Lydia Smith (12)

My Baby Sister And Friends

My baby sister looks so cute
my baby sister's an angel
whenever she gets the remote she presses mute
but sometimes she's a devil.

My friends are very funny
my friends are very sweet
and whenever it's sunny
we all get together to have a treat.

My baby sister is the best of us all
now she's started to make faces
just to tell you she's not very tall
by the way her name's Ansaria.

My friends are nice
my baby sister is cute
my friends know my baby sister
and she knows them, but do you?

Saarah Bibi (10)

Who Is It?

She's as noisy as an elephant,
As shy as a mouse,
As pretty as a pony,
As tall as a house.

She's as clever as an eagle,
As lazy as TV,
As messy as an artist,
As crazy as can be.

She's as playful as a puppy,
As busy as a bee,
As funny as a clown,
Could you guess?
It's me!

Amber Theckston (10)

Someone Special

Whenever I need some grub in my tum,
The person I ask is my mum.
The food she makes is really great,
So that's why she's my best mate.

Whenever we go somewhere abroad,
It's always somewhere that we can afford.
The places she takes me to are great,
So that's why she's my best mate.

Whenever I'm down it's not for long,
'Cause Mom makes me feel that I belong.
The help she gives me is really great,
So that's why she's my best mate.

Wherever we go there's someone beside me,
That someone beside me is special to me.
She encourages me in my art,
So that's why she's got a place in my heart.

Liam Culbertson (12)

Grandad

My favourite person to me
is my grandad called Terry,
we go out in the sunshine,
and also when it rains,
we have a shared hobby,
which happens to be trains.

He's one in a million without a doubt,
when I need anything he will
get his credit card out.
Many places we go to, many places we see,
our favourite place is definitely Whitby.

The adventures we go on have always been great,
I love my grandad, he is my mate!

Zoe Purnell Newman (11)

Amber

Amber is my very best friend
I hope our friendship never ends
She cheers me up when I feel blue
When I'm unhappy she brings me through

At school we always play together
We never argue, *never ever*
Since we met in Year 1
We've always had so much fun

When we get together out of school
We normally go to the swimming pool
We splash around and have lots of fun
And then we lay out in the sun

When we get older and drift apart
I'll still have Amber in my heart
I hope we keep in touch together
As I want to know her forever and ever.

Olivia Connelly (8)

Special Mum!

My mum, the mum of all
She hopes she's the best of all
She cleans, she helps
She messes around
But I know she's the mum of all.

She takes me everywhere
To see the world but I don't care
That's why my mum's there.

My favourite person is the best
She begins with m and ends in m
There's a u in the middle
But guess what, she's always there
Watching over me.

Victoria Murley (10)

96

My Favourite Person . . .

She's always there to cheer me up
And greets me with a smile.
She does my hair in curly buns -
Which usually takes a while!

We've had lots of adventures
To foreign lands and more:
Trodden land on horseback
And floated far from shore.

I know I have a friend I trust,
With her I won't feel blue.
I know she is a brilliant friend,
I hope I am one too!

I love my best friend, Laura.
Even when we're grey and old,
I know that we'll be best of friends
That's what the future holds.

Justine Gormley (10)

My Best Friend, Gizmo

(In loving memory of Gizmo)

Although he's a dog,
He was a best friend to me,
All cuddly and soft
Like a toy teddy.

We played together
Each lovely day,
Sharing secrets
In our own kind of way.

Now it is night,
Playtime's at an end.
Gizmo was great,
He was my best friend.

Charley West (12)

My Best Friends

My best friend, Ellie,
Takes me with her to places.
My best friend is Ellie,
We both have smiling faces.

My best friend is Isabella,
We go on trips together.
My best friend is Isabella,
We never forget each other.

My best friend is Aitana,
Although she lives in Spain.
My best friend is Aitana,
Sometimes she can be insane!

I went to Butlins with Ellie,
Isabella often invites me to sleepovers,
Aitana and me play in the park together,
So this is a dedication for my bestest friends!

Phoebe Linane (10)

My Best Friend

My best friend is my pony
I call him Scruffy Smurf
He's 21 years old
But is still as fit as a fiddle

He changes colour every season
And he is very, very chunky
If he eats too much grass
I'm afraid he might explode!

My perfect pony does everything
He jumps very well
We've won lots and lots of prizes
And I'm very proud of him.

Chloe Muggeridge (10)

My Favourite Person!

When I was younger
It made me wonder,
If I would get
Another sister or pet.

Sometimes she's good,
Sometimes she's bad,
She makes me happy,
She makes me sad.

We play together,
We laugh and sing,
These are just a few
Of our favourite things.

I'm really glad
But sometimes sad,
She is to stay the same way
So that is why I wrote today!

Chantal Brown (10)

Jessie, Our Cat!

J essie, our cat, is full of cattitude
E xcitable and very mischievous
S oft and extremely cuddly
S uper at catching mice
I nquisitive and very intelligent
E scapes through the bedroom window at night

O ur cat is very friendly
U nder the shed she gets covered in spiders' webs
R eally kind and loving is our cat

C omes through the bedroom in the morning and purrs loudly
A ll of the cats in the lane are Jessie's best friends
T umbles and rolls over if you tickle her tummy, and miaows.

Chloë Emmett (9)

Thank You, Nelson!

My favourite person is Nelson Mandela,
He brought different people together.
How he fought and fought for our rights,
In him he had courage and might.

If he had never been alive,
We'd still be fighting day and night.
Now we can mix people whatsoever,
Sharing relationships that last forever.

I picture us strong friends,
Having a belief that doesn't end.
'Something inside so strong',
That's the name of our favourite song.

I thank Nelson Mandela,
Now we don't have to live in pressure,
As we can share our troubles with our friends.
Nelson Mandela is my favourite person!

Rasha Vadamootoo (10)

Miss Carver

My favourite person to write about
Is Miss Carver without a doubt.
She was my teacher in infant school,
I liked her a lot, she's very cool.

Miss Carver was always happy and polite,
She always taught us wrong from right.
Miss Carver listened to us when we spoke,
She laughed with us and made us joke.

I've started high school now you see,
And teachers will be strict to me.
I'll miss Miss Carver from my primary,
But I'll always be glad that she taught me.

Gemma Middlehurst (11)

I Have A Little Brother

I have a little brother
I was there when he was born
He has a lovely smile
Which he seems to do all the while!

I love my little brother
I'm glad to have him around
We both like listening to music
When we dance and jump around.

I'm glad I've got a brother
He will always be my friend
We'll always be together
Best friends till the end.

Thank you little brother
I just wanted you to know
The enjoyment that you bring to me
Is the best thing I have known.

Joshua Myers (7)

The One And Only!

I love my granny,
She bakes me brownies,
But if she doesn't make them
It gives me the frownies.

On a sunny day
She'll bring me lemonade,
Together we shall sit
In the cool shade.

On a winter's evening
She makes a cup of tea,
And a chocolate biscuit
Especially for me!

Danielle Preskey (11)

My Favourite Person

I have a favourite person
Her name is Juliet
She is the world's greatest mum
Always up for loads of fun

She helps me through school
With homework and with projects
I could not live without her
And the times filled with laughter

Her cakes are really scrummy
The chilli is delicious
I would not miss her Bolognese
Her chicken is a whizzer

You must have realised now
I love her very much
Her kindness and support
Keeps me going when it's tough.

Graciela Niembro (10)

Mummy

I miss you in the morning
When you go to work,
But know you need to go
So we can all have a perk.

We love it when you come home
So we can see your smiling face
Because you know home
Is a happy place.

I give you lots of kisses
When you walk through the door,
But if it was up to me, Mummy,
I would give you *more and more!*

Katie Barrett (9)

102

My Favourite Person

My favourite person has the strangest laugh.
It's loud and weird and funny.
His gleaming smile and bright brown eyes
make the whole world really sunny.

My favourite person strums perfect chords
whenever he plays guitar.
I wish I could play as well as him,
he's my shiny star.

When my favourite person hums all day
it drives me round the bend.
But no matter how I scream or shout
he'll always be my friend.

My favourite person's everything.
He's lovely, sweet and kind.
He's my little brother
and he's also very mine.

Lauren Hughes (13)

My Grandma

My grandma is the greatest,
My grandma is the best,
She always loves to smile,
Which makes me smile too!

My grandma is the greatest,
Someone you'll always adore,
If you're looking for a friend,
You've found who you're looking for!

My grandma is the greatest,
If you met her you would know
She's the greatest grandma ever,
And it's something I can show!

Bethany Quinn (11)

Pritt Sticks

I didn't always like him,
he seemed a little smart,
but something about this
boy was tugging at my heart.

The teacher told us to work
and he was paired with me,
I feared it would be disastrous
but it turned out not to be.

There began our friendship
and then it grew and grew,
now we are two Pritt Sticks,
stuck together like glue.

There's something vital missing
when he's absent or off sick,
if I could choose a friend for life,
he's the one I'd pick.

Lauren Dowling (10)

What You Mean To Me

How can I describe what you mean to me?
The most beautiful flower standing alone
Unique, thriving in impossible conditions
All other wonders diminished by your beauty

Orange strands of fire reaching out from the sky
Curling, twisting, engulfing the world
So dazzling my wide eyes are blinded
Yet the angelic scene you provide shatters my worry

All these stunning wonders of the world
They shine from your eyes
Lighting up the universe
And that's what you mean to me.

Shona Lavelle (14)

My Nana

I love spending time with my nana,
She really is super nice,
She has a Jack Russell called Max,
Who doesn't like to catch mice.

She spends a lot of time knitting
And is a brilliant cook.
Her favourite programme is Emmerdale
And she loves reading books.

Nana has sparkling blue eyes
And a head full of curly white hair.
She's always there for a cuddle
And I know she really cares.

I can speak to Nana about anything,
She helps me with my tests.
She is my favourite person,
Nana is absolutely the best.

Courtney Emblem (10)

My Best Friend Carys

Carys is my best friend because
she is clever and kind,
thinks about other people
and not just herself,
she also helps you
with your spelling.

Carys always smiles and
cheers you up,
when you are feeling left out,
lonely or down.

Carys is my best friend because
she is the best.

Taylor Davies (11)

My Favourite Person

My favourite person
Is a good friend of mine.
She always makes me laugh and smile
And is always good, friendly and kind.

She isn't at all shy,
She would stand up for me,
She doesn't back down from a challenge,
Challenge her and you would see.

When we get into trouble at school
She gets the blame.
She is quite mad about guinea pigs,
She drives us all insane.

This person is my best mate,
She is really fabby.
I still love her lots
And her name is Abbi.

Amber Chawner (12)

My Mum

My mum is my favourite person,
She's gentle, kind and fun,
She says we're lovely daughters,
And one very special son.

If we get hurt she'll give us a hug,
She won't shout even when we break her mug,
If we don't listen and we touch,
My mum will still love us so much.

My mum is my favourite person,
I think she's number one,
She's not just kind to us kids,
She's kind to everyone!

Chloe Bent (11)

My Only Hero

When it's raining it's such a miserable day,
But you make the sun come out and everything is OK.
You make me feel loved, wonderful and special,
You're kind, caring and ever so gentle.

You're my only hero.

Spending money and spoiling me,
You tell me to be who I wanna be.
Messing around, being really funny,
Going abroad where it is very sunny.

You're my only hero.

I may be growing up, but I'm still your little girl,
With you by my side I will be sent to Heaven, not Hell.
Because of you my life has been so happy,
Ever since I was a baby in a nappy.

That's why Dad, you're my hero.

Caitlin Beebe (11)

My Dad

My daddy's the best
He's never taken to the test
He's a tall man
And he can flip a pancake in a pan

He is a really good man
With a big hand
He's a really caring dad
And he's never bad

He is the best
Don't forget he is
Never taken to the
 Test!

My dad is the best person in the world!

Mohammed Lukeman Pathan (11)

My Best Friend

My best friend is Jess
And I think she's the best.

When me and Jess play out together,
We always have the best time ever,
Whatever the weather.

Whenever I'm feeling down in the dumps,
Jess will be there, I know that she will care.

Jess can always make me smile,
Even if it's just for a little while.

I'm writing this poem in blue for you,
'Cause I know it's your favourite colour.

Wherever you go,
I would like you to know
That you will always be,
My best friend!

Tia Foxon (11)

All About My Family

My mum makes me very good food every day
And helps me do my homework,
Takes me to school.

My dad bought me a toy
And helps me with my homework.
Sometimes he makes me food,
He takes me to school.

My sister does my hair.
When my mum goes out,
She looks after me.

My brother bought me a toy
For my birthday,
And bought me a phone.

Rasidatu Bisuga (7)

My Favourite Brother

The first day he came into the house,
He was quiet as a mouse,
When I held him in my arms,
I felt his soft little palms,
Everyone was happy I helped with the nappy,
Now he is eight,
He is my favourite mate,
We always play,
With his favourite toy clay,
I look out for him at school,
He thinks he is cool,
He looks up at me,
I always make him tea,
He is my little bro,
One day he will be a racing pro,
Rich and famous like Simon Cowell,
But will he remember me?

Halimah Shahban (11)

Messi Rocks

Messi is a football star
All he does is shoot and score
You have to be tough to get past him
He's better than Cristiano Ronaldo
He puts him to shame
He loves to use his skills in matches
But he never means to show off.

Of course he's Messi
He is a mighty football player
He plays for BCF
All they are is the greatest football team
Apart from me
The greatest player of all times
Ben Campbell.

Ben Campbell (8)

My Daddy Is My Hero

My daddy is my hero,
He's always good and kind,
My daddy is my hero,
He's there for me all the time,
My daddy is my hero,
He takes me everywhere,
My daddy is my hero,
He's always strong and fair,
My daddy is my hero,
He always makes me smile,
My daddy is my hero,
He goes the extra mile,
My daddy is my hero,
He loves me more and more,
My daddy is my hero,
I don't mean to be a bore,
But, my daddy is my hero.

Sophie Barnwell (8)

What Makes Me Glad

Purring round the garden
In search of a little mouse.
It makes Mum and Dad so very cross
When she brings them in the house.

A silver tabby she is, so what?
She's still a funny friend.
Like the time she slept in my sister's cot
And made muddy paw prints on my bed.

She follows me almost everywhere,
And when I'm feeling sad
She cuddles up into my arms,
And that's what makes me glad.

Esmé Partridge (9)

My Grandad (1938-2008)

Best hugger
Chief gardener
World traveller
Largest smiler
Question giver
Answer knower
Homework helper
Ship fixer
Flower waterer
Voodoo maker
Hippo chaser
Traffic light builder
Samurai warrior
Engine constructor
Chandelier worker
Navy doer
Country goer.

James Dodd (10)

Tania

She's kind, she's nice,
Scared of mice,
Has a cat,
Whose name is Mat.

Caring and sweet,
Likes a treat,
Clever and tall,
Goes to the mall.

Hungry as always,
Walks near the roadways,
Name rhymes with lasagne,
Her name is Tania!

Ruksana Akter (11)

My Favourite Person

My favourite person is my mum,
She is a crazy dancer, opera singer, shopaholic
And a cooking crazy type of mum.
She is always the star of the show,
She is a cooking, cleaning, always ironing type of mum.
She is a race to school, handbag type of person.
She is a chatty, giggly, scary lipstick type of mum
And she always pops like a popcorn machine.
She is a posh, mindbobbling fancy food type of person.
She is a cool, groovy and funky type of lady.
She is a coffee crazy, whoops-a-daisy type of lady.
She is a sweet dream, party type of lady.
She is a colourful rainbow.
She is a summer kind of lady, always sunny
And a flip-flop kind of lady.
She's a time for bed, adventurous type of lady.
That's why she's my favourite person!

Niamh Scanlon (9)

My Nan

When she opens the door,
The whole room lights up.
The smile on her face,
It glows like the stars in the night sky.
Her twinkling green eyes sparkle
As if they were the fresh dew in the morning.
She supports me in whatever I do,
Whether it's sports or music.
She needn't shower me with many gifts
Because I know a great big hug
Shows that she loves me.
If I give her one back, she knows I love her too.

Rebecca Andrews (11)

My Cat, Garfield

My cat, Garfield, is a rascal.
He sneaks upstairs on my bed,
Instead I put him in his bed.
The cheeky rebel loves to play,
Up the curtains and in the washing basket all day.

His fur is ginger with different tones of orange and gold.
He's bright like the sunshine.
When he pounces he is bold.
He has stripes like a tiger,
His eyes are a smoky emerald-green.
He looks fierce, but isn't mean.

When he wants to go out he waits
By the small and boxy hall.
He's a fluffball that moults a lot
I rush to give him a brush.
My cat, Garfield, is my favourite pet.

Katie Tart (11)

My Funny Bunny

I love my bunny's long ears
Because they're like my wet tears.
I love my bunny's little nose
Because it doesn't smell like my brother's toes.
I love my bunny's tail
Because it's nothing like a slimy snail.
I love my bunny's whiskers,
Because they're not sharp, dangerous killers.
I love my bunny's eyes
Because they're like big black flies.
I love my bunny because it's so funny,
But I have to give you back, bunny, and move on.

Amy Hagan (10)

Tinkerbell

Tinkerbell is really nice,
She sometimes even eats rice,
But it's good that she doesn't have lice.

Tinkerbell's type is really rare,
I think it's nice how she does her hair.
She's so pretty and she really does care.

Tinkerbell doesn't like to fly that low,
But she does like to put on a comedy show,
Because she is a fairy, she has such a tiny toe.

Tinkerbell's okay when it's night,
When it's morning, out comes the light.
She never wants to put up a fight,
But Tinkerbell doesn't drink any Sprite.

So who is my best friend?
Tinkerbell!

Sophie Lambrou (10)

Ginny

To jump with
And ride with
And be by my side with

To trick with
And try with
And show you're alive with

To play with
And stay with
Forever and a day with

To fly with
And sigh with
Occasionally cry with.

My pony.

Elizabeth Pope (11)

114

My Dog Spike

I have a dog
his name is Spike

He's always trying
to ride my bike

He likes the park
but he always barks

He loves his bath
and makes me laugh

He howls and yells
and makes bad smells

My mum, she shouts
and kicks him out

He drives my dad around the bend
but he'll always be my bestest friend.

Francesca Riley (10)

Super Gran

My grandma is a sapphire, luminous jewel,
And I think she's super cool.
Everything my grandma does
Makes me feel pleasant and full of fuzz.
When we grab a chair and do our complicated puzzles,
My tickled pink heart feels full of her blissful cuddles.

All her appreciative grandchildren come round for Friday tea,
You can see my grandma's face is full of glee.
Although me and my cousin Sam are continuously in trouble,
My grandma says, 'Leave them alone,' and gives us a content cuddle.

She's like a luminous star that's gleaming above
And she shares and gives so much inspirational love.
There's no one in the colossal universe that is as lucky as me,
Because I have the most incomparable grandma that there can ever be.

Bethany Horbury (11)

My Mum

My mum is number one,
She doesn't like the sun.

When I am hurt,
She sends an alert.

When I am sad,
She makes me glad.

When I walk in a puddle,
She gives me a cuddle.

In May,
She likes to play.

When I play my guitar,
She says I'm a star.

That's my mum,
She's so much fun!

Elisha Tong (10)

The Stig

My favourite person is 'The Stig'.
He drives like the wind,
Is awesome and shows no fear!
I never miss an episode of Top Gear.

I'm only 10 and have
Passed my MSA driving test.
When I grow up
I want to be just like him.
He's fantastic, in fact the best!

All I need now is to get sponsors
To help me along the way.
My dream is to meet 'The Stig' someday!
I go lots to practise my racing line,
One day hopefully his job will be mine.

Lewis Crowther (10)

116

Lovely Lizzie

Lizzie and me are there for each other
And caring for one another.

Sharing and playing, we have so much fun
And chatting, there in the sun.

We both have parties all around,
Playing sleeping lions, *shhh* . . . not a sound.

She took me camping and we had a blast,
We were so energetic that we went to sleep fast.

Me and Lizzie tried to stay up late,
But it was only half-past eight!

When we fell asleep,
There was not a peep.

Now it's time to say goodbye,
See you next time, bye-bye.

Charlotte Colne (10)

My Cat, Bruno

M y best friend is Bruno
Y ou would love my cat

F iery red is his fur
R acing round the flat
I f he's in the snow
E ven in the rain
N ever mind the mess
D ifferent cats would be plain

B runo's like a yo-yo
R unning up and down
U nderneath and through and low
N ever seen him frown
O range is his fur and Bruno is his name
        no other cat could ever be the same.

Heidi Burgess (12)

Father, Oh Father!

C'mon Dad, don't wash the clothes,
We're already late, come, let's go.

Please Dad, get up, come and play,
It'll only be a two-second game.

Hurry up Dad, pick up the pace,
You don't need to worry about your shoelace.

C'mon Dad, pass the ball,
Oh Dad, you could have scored.

Hurry up Dad, I'm bleeding like crazy,
This is no time to be lazy.

Oh Dad, stop frolicking with Mother,
Can't you just think about Ayman, my brother?

My dad is one of a kind,
But you wouldn't want to see his darker side.

Khalil McGuinness (11)

My Favourite Person

My favourite person right now is Martin Luther King.
Through words he won a war, no guns needed,
no lives wasted,
all people, every colour, treated the same.
Marched marches,
led the people,
helped the good,
taught the bad where they went wrong.
Not one girl, not one lad,
but everyone and all.
His famous words, 'I have a dream.'
My dream, 'Peace for all.'

Patrick McGourty (11)

My Sister

With black, glossy hair,
And shimmering eyes,
She never despairs,
She never cries.
How she does it,
It's a wonder to me,
But I love her,
And she loves me.

Comforting and calm,
As gentle as a hymn,
As peaceful as a psalm,
My favourite person deep within,
How she does it,
It's a wonder to me,
But I love her,
And she loves me.

Sara Atri (10)

All About You

Her name is Gemma,
Her favourite colour is blue.
Her favourite show on Disney Channel
Is the Suite Life of Zack and Cody.
Her birthday is on the 12th of March
And she was born in 2002.
We take her to parties sometimes,
Sometimes she sleeps over at my house.
Me and her have joined-up birthdays.
Gemma is annoyed because
We always get the same presents.
I don't really care
Because it is better than nothing.
Whenever we are together we have fun,
She always helps me and she is really funny.

Ellie Doyle (7)

My Special Mom

My mom is the best,
She deserves a big rest,
Mom, put up your feet,
I will get you a treat,
Sit back, read this now,
Let's hope you go *wow!*

My mom is the favourite one, without a doubt,
That's what this poem is all about,
You take me here, there and everywhere,
I feel I should pay you taxi fare,
Mom, you just don't stop,
You're always trying to beat the clock,
You're loving, kind, thoughtful and caring,
Myself, my sister, you and Dad all sharing,
The list could just go on and on,
That's why you're such a *special mom!*

Brooke Holland (9)

My Favourite Person

My favourite person tends to be
Not one of my friends or family
Or even a stranger I don't know - indeed!
For if I chose one
The others may care
Which would leave me feeling very unfair.
The person I choose
Should be close to me
And know as much about me
As I do you see.
And so I choose, me, myself and I
I know what you're thinking
This isn't a lie
Because how can I love others
And not I?

Kanchelli Iddrisu (12)

120

My Favourite Person

Like a Roman candle we all stare in awe,
She will come to rescue me and bring me back ashore.

She tells me great stories of places she has been
And hoovers the carpets so they'll be nice and clean.
If I cry she will wipe the tears from my eyes,
She is like an owl, exceedingly clever and wise.
As brave as a lion, but without the bite,
She teaches me life's lessons so I will do right.
Buying me new clothes so I will stay cool,
She's also a perfect taxi for taking me to school.
Making cooked breakfast, dinner and tea,
However busy she is, she always has time for me.
When I've had a shower, she blow-dries my hair,
When I'm eating chocolate, with her I will share.
She'll always be my favourite because she's my mum,
If I shout for help, she will always come.

Emily Davies (11)

My Favourite Person, Elly

My friend is called Elly,
Her feet are very smelly.
We drive each other round the bend,
We get together in the end.
We miss her horse, Honey,
She was very funny.
Then she had Kizzy,
She kept us all busy.
The horse was quite frightening,
She ran like lightning.
Elly is very small
And I am very tall.
People stare
But we don't care
Because we make a good pair.

Lucy Mousley (10)

Mollie, The Border Collie!

My best friend
Is my nan's dog.
She's a border collie
And her name is Mollie.
When I go to visit my nan
Mollie is waiting for me,
Her tail is wagging,
At the door she's jumping.
Mollie's fur is lush and soft to touch,
She knows I love her very much.

I've taught Mollie lots of tricks,
High five paw, which hand, are just a few.
Find the treat, hide-and-seek too.
Mollie gives me cuddles when I'm very sad,
She even cuddles me when I'm bad.
That's why Mollie's my best friend.

Stacey Webster (9)

Gingerlicious!

I love the way your ginger hair glows in the sun!
I love the way I'd spend all my money on you in a flash, just to see one tiny
smile on your face.
I love the way you can make me laugh, frown, smile or even cry at the click of
a finger.
But most of all I love the way that when we are alone I get to see a side of you
that not many other people get to see.
A side that gets frightened.
A side that has feelings.
A side that even cries now and then.
A side that's human!
I love you dearly my brother Tom,
It's fair to say that on me you've made a deep impression.
So please don't ignore me whatever you do,
Because, my brother Tom, you're my favourite person it's true!

Lauren Spencer Stabbins (12)

My Favourite Person

My favourite person wears big black clogs
And sits on logs,
Even though she is two feet tall,
She can really whack the footie ball.
Her hair is blonde, always in a bun,
She loves to sit under the sun.

My favourite person has a ginger cat,
But sadly he's as blind as a bat.
He walks around with his head so high,
But other cats look down and cry.

My favourite person does gymnastics,
She can even do seven backflips.
She is so strong and never wrong,
She hates the doorbell when it goes *ding-dong*.

My favourite person is imaginary!

Emily Dodds (11)

The True Poem, My Favourite Person

When my grandma died;
I screamed, I cried.
I miss my grandma loads.
The plural of loud is louds.
My grandma is in the clouds.
She is important to me.
She always had a pan
To feed the whole clan.
My grandma was the best,
She never wanted to rest.
She was glad to be able to see,
She also drank tea.
My grandma is a favourite person of mine,
This has all come from my heart.
Oh yeah, she liked treacle tart.

Aimée Kelly (9)

My Dad And Me

My dad loves me and I love him,
Together we're a fabulous pair,
Making things fair and square,
For the games we like to play,
Of every hour of every day.

Me and my dad have two bikes,
Lucky because biking is what we like.
We also both like walking,
Walking on hills while talking.

Both of us go everywhere,
Everywhere, here and there.
Just the two of us is just fine
To make a happy and fantastic time.

As you can see we will always be together,
Always be together forever and ever.

Jasmine Turner (10)

My Best Friend

She's bubbly, friendly and full of fun
Together we have great adventures in the sun
We love to chat and sing and dance
Where in the playground you'll see us prance
Whenever I'm sad, she makes me smile
And then we go and play a while
We both love make-up, we both love fashion
You could say they are our passion
She has green eyes and hair so blonde
It's great to have this friendship bond
My favourite person has to be
My friend at school, my best friend Niamh.

Cara Smith (8)

My Guinea Pig

When I named my guinea pig Lucy
She was so small and sweet
But since then she's grown bigger
Boy does my friend eat!

She loves munching on grass
But when it comes to muesli
She says she'll pass.

When she's crunching on carrots
That's what I like to see
The thing I don't like
Is when she misses and crunches me.

During the day her coat shines in the sun
And her eyes are bright
But I often wonder what
She does in her cage at night.

Shannon Logan (10)

My Family

My name is Reece Wilson and I'm 7 years old,
I'm actually quite clever - or so I've been told.
I live with my 2 sisters, Mum and my dad,
I'm usually very happy and not often sad.
My granny and granda live down the lane
So I go to visit to keep Mummy sane!
My sister and me go to school every day,
We work really hard then have a play.
It's really quite hard to think who I like best,
In fact thinking about it is like doing a test.
My family love me now that I'm big, and when I was small,
So I would have to say that my family are my favourite people of all.

Reece Wilson (7)

125

My Favourite Person

My baby sister climbs up the stairs and down the stairs
And slaps me on my face.

My baby sister claps her hands and rubs her toes
When she's angry she hits me on the nose.

My baby sister likes to splash in the bath
My mum wraps her up and gets her ready in a flash.

My baby sister cries and screams
And has a tantrum when she wants to eat.

My baby sister explores the room
She crawls around pulling out phone wires
Picks up the tiniest objects and puts them in her mouth.

My baby sister has had enough for today
She rubs her eyes and cuddles Mum
Ready to sleep for another day.

Mehboob Kassam (9)

Too Many Friends

I have two best friends,
One very well trained dog
And another trustworthy friend,
But I have to focus on both, who?

Shannon is one of my best friends,
And she's always going to be round the bends,
Just one step and she'll be there,
Waiting for some kind of care.

Next there's Bootsy, my dog,
Who loves to play all day with logs.
He's cute and fun,
And we both hate it when the day is done.

The two of my best friends have been with me all my life
And also one more - my mum!

Amy Davies (11)

My Grandma

With a smile and grey hair,
I know she'll be there.
Through the thick and the thin,
Making me grin.
From the moment I was born,
From dusk then to dawn.
Loves to cook,
And read a good book.
Likes the colour red,
'Careful!' she says.
Grandma, mother and wife,
Important in my life.
This poem comes from the heart,
Like Picasso's astounding art.
I'm her biggest fan,
This is my gran!

Jessie Lam (11)

My Favourite Person

My favourite person is my mother,
Who always loved and cared for me,
She would sing sweet rhymes every night,
As she bounced me on her knee.

She'd read a fairy tale and tuck me in bed,
She'd say goodnight and kiss me on my head.
When I get nightmares she says, 'It's alright,
You're my little princess, there's no need to fright.'

She helps me when I'm studying,
So my marks will be the best,
She prepares me and encourages me,
Before I take those tests.

I don't care what people say
Because my mum's my favourite person *every day!*

Abreen Rebello (11)

Super Mom

Mom, you're a wonderful mother,
So gentle, yet so strong.
The many ways you show you care
Always make me feel I belong.
You're patient when I'm foolish,
You give guidance when I cook,
It seems you can do almost anything;
You're the master of every task.
You're a dependable source of comfort,
You're my cushion when I fall,
You help in times of trouble,
You support me whenever I call.
I love you more than you know,
You have my loyal respect.
If I had my choice of mothers,
You'd be the one I would select.

Yasir Jamah (8)

My Favourite Person

My favourite person is my mam
She always makes me laugh
Except when she's mad at me
And acts like a psychopath

She listens to me read a book
If I can't find a toy she'll help me look
She tidies away my mess
And never loves me any less

She embarrassed me at school
Because it is not cool
When in the yard she wants a kiss
I turn my head so she'll miss

But I know no matter what will be
My mam is always there for me!

Anthony Teasdale (10)

128

My Sister

I'm thinking this person's the best
I'm thinking this person's so cool
I'm thinking this person's a legend
I however, know nothing at all
It could be the heart inside me
It could be the brain in my head
It could be the soul besides me
Or it could be the role model by which I was led
They say only time can tell
But by now I know this person so well
I've lived with her since I was zero
Now she has become my hero
I couldn't have done it without her
I couldn't have survived myself
And that's why this person's so worthy
You should pat her on the back yourself.

Ben Doyle (13)

My Mum

My mum is fair,
But she's never square.
My mum is lovely,
She's not at all ugly.
My mum is kind
And has an open mind.
My mum is nice,
As cool as ice.
My mum is top
And she likes pop.
There will never be another one
Like *my* mum!

Jordan Hollies (11)

My Favourite Person

God made us sisters
So we can be best of friends,
To be there for one another
And sisters till the end.
I thank the Lord for bringing her down to Earth
For she's the one I trust and care.
I tell her everything,
Even when I'm scared.
We occasionally argue,
But that's what sisters do,
But having you as my sister
Means more to me than it does to you.
I would never think of trading you,
I will never let you go,
Just always remember you can trust me
As our friendship starts to grow.

Georgia Osei (11)

My Friend, Niamh

She is my best friend, we don't pretend
We play with each other
Neither of us would have any other
We have known each other for six years
You wouldn't believe how much mayhem we did
When we were in reception
We used to make a lot of corrections
We'd hide behind the dinner lady's back
To see if she would notice our laugh
Niamh is great, she's my best mate
She's never late, she loves to create
Now goodbye, I'm late for my mate.

Morgan Partridge (9)

My Brother

My brother is like my mother
because he bosses me about.
He rants and he rages.
We listen to him shout.
We leave the room to calm him down,
otherwise he will carry on being the silly clown.
He acts like an animal in the zoo
until my auntie tells him what to do.
He will then calm down
and play on his PS3
while Mum and me make the tea.
He is now like the brother I know,
but wait, hang on, here we go!
He thinks he's the boss because he is 13
but we know better, Mum and me.
I say, 'Calm down it's time for tea.'

Sasha Yilmaz (8)

Me And My Dog

Me and my dog like to play around,
I have a lot of adventures with that hound.
We go through the bushes and the trees,
We lie outside when there's a nice cool breeze.
We always like to go to the park,
Where all the little doggies bark.
You always used to chase after your ball
And whenever it was sunny you'd lie in the hall.
When I was three, you were four,
When I tried to walk you, you pulled me through the door.
Now you are 11 and I am 10,
We have had so many adventures again and again.

Natasha Paynter (11)

My Dad

He's about five foot eight in his stocking feet,
His hair's the texture of a brillo pad but always very neat,
He's very competitive and hates to be beaten on the Wii,
Even if his competitor happens to be me!
He is without doubt the best at DIY,
He has a strange garage full of tools and gadgets and that's no lie,
He shares with me all that he knows,
I rake the grass cuttings as he mows,
We grow our own plants, veg and flowers,
In his greenhouse we spend hours,
He winds me up with his tricks and his jokes,
He has me in stitches, such a funny bloke,
He adores my mum, that's clear to see,
There is nothing he wouldn't do for my sister and me,
I realise that I'm such a lucky lad,
Cos there's none that can compare to my fantastic dad.

Jacob Gaskell (10)

My Favourite Person 2009

Remembering my nanny
Who is my favourite person
And I also miss dearly
As she passed away.

I remember her
Reading me stories when I was younger
And having lots of laughs and giggles too.

But Nanny would hug me and say
I was her very special granddaughter,
But now she's gone,
I miss her.

Bethany Thomson (11)

Caring Angels

Parents are angels that care about me
They take me on trips like to the sea
My loving parents look out for me no matter where I go
And they always teach me everything they know
They clean my cuts and hug me when I cry
They make me laugh until my tears are dry
Parents are stars from the midnight sky
Whenever they're ill, I bake them their favourite pie
Parents are far more precious than gold
I always do as I'm told
They try so hard to make me see
But I barely listen, I only want to be free
A parent's love is everlasting
Which is why they are the people that I am appreciating
Dad is cuddly and Mum is understanding
Those gifts are the ones I am always adoring.

Siti Mohd Fauzi (11)

My Mum

A favourite person,
is someone you love,
my favourite person is my mum,
she always puts a smile on my face,
helping me when I'm down.

I love my mum that is why,
she's my favourite person,
I couldn't be without her,
she is kind and funny,
and always giving us hugs.

My mum is my favourite person.

Emily Grace Coe (11)

My Favourite Person

My favourite person used to be Kitty,
But now she's left me, what a pity.
My favourite person might be Dad,
But yesterday he drove me mad.
My favourite person could be Mum,
But today she wasn't any fun.
My brother Joseph isn't bad,
At tea he spoiled it, how sad, how sad.
It could be Kiera, my friend from school,
But Amber from swimming is really cool.
Lottie, my cat, I gave her my love,
But now she's up in Heaven above.
There's no one that I've mentioned that I would like to lose,
I don't know who the best is, it's really hard to choose.
It's hard to pick a favourite, that is plain to see,
I'll just be friends with everyone, then they'll be friends with me!

Emily Lampon (9)

My Good Mum

My favourite person is my mum,
She's my friend, but still tells me off when I'm naughty.
My mum's always there for me when I need her
Just like my secret blanky I had when I was young.
A little bit older, rough around the edge
But soft and cuddly and strong.

I know I can tell my mum anything
And it wouldn't bother her.
Mom gives advice, I don't always listen.
I should 'cause Mum's usually right.

I love my mum 'cause she's mine!

William Wright (10)

134

That's What I Like About Her

When I see Blessing, my friend,
I know our friendship will never end.
When she smiles,
You can see it for miles,
That's what I like about her.

When we are playing together,
I know our friendship will last forever.
When I am sad,
She makes me feel glad,
That's what I like about her.

When Blessing is with me,
I know we'll laugh, hee-hee,
She's always my friend,
With a helping hand to lend,
That's what I like about her.

Rhianna Thurgood (9)

Buster My Dog

B uster you are so cute,
U nbelievably intelligent and smart,
S ometimes you can annoy me,
T ogether we make a great team though.
E very time I am sad you're there,
R ealising my pain and helping me to repair.

M uch fun I have with you,
Y ou are my *best friend*.

D eclaring my love for you is easy,
O ften a cuddle is all I need.
G od what a wonderful animal you are.

Kaylem D'Costa (11)

My Auntie Sophie

My favourite person is my auntie, Sophie
She buys me things every day
Some days she's mean to me
But she loves me in every way

She's also a baronet
Who plays beside the hearth
And likes to play the clarinet
Whilst sitting in the bath

At half-past four every day
We run outside to talk and play

I love it when she tries to do the moonwalk
The way she sings and dances and does her silly talk

Some days when I'm sad we cuddle up together
And I think to myself, *she's the greatest auntie ever.*

Celica Robinson (11)

My Best Friend - Erin May Harris

My favourite person
Is my best friend, Erin.
Whenever me and Erin want a laugh
I always call her 'Erin Perrin'.

She's clever, she's friendly,
She's my best friend in this country.
I remember, at school,
She sometimes said, 'Lunchie!'

She's my favourite person of 2009,
She's gonna be my favourite person
Nearly all of the time!

Laura Mills (11)

My Puppy

Snuggly, cuddly, bundle of fun,
Playing in the summer sun.

Running here and rushing there.
Lolloping, frolicking everywhere.

Toys all strewn across the grass,
Destroying everything in its path.

Exhausted now, becoming calm,
Time to relax in your arms.

Excited times drive you round the bend,
But look at me now, Man's best friend!

Katie Arnott (11)

My Favourite Person

My favourite person is my mum.
I like her because she is always around.

My favourite person is my nan.
I like her because she gives me lots of sweets once in a while.

My favourite person is my friend Jessica.
I like her because she is funny.

My favourite person is my sister Rebekah.
I like her because she is fun.

I have four different favourite people,
So I couldn't choose one!

Chloe-Leigh Nash (8)

My Marvellous Mum

My mum is the best,
By far more effective than the rest.

Her talent shines like the sun,
She will always be my mum.

My mum is a remarkable cook,
Carries more knowledge than a book.

Her love for me is immense,
Without her life wouldn't make sense.

Yes, even a small kid knows
Without mums, this world is nothing.

Edward Gokmen (10)

The Best Mum Ever

My favourite
person is my mum
she is the best of
all the rest
even when she is
stressed, she
rocks my world
and my heart
I love her so, my
mum is my best
friend.

Roman Burke (9)

My Favourite Person Is . . .

My favourite person is not human, she's small
And she has four legs, that's all.
My favourite person is such a nuisance, she's a laugh!
And she ain't as tall as a giraffe.
My favourite person is unique in so many ways
And she's cute every day, every day!
My favourite person is always interested in what I do,
She even helped me write this for you!
My favourite person is my best ever friend,
And that friend is my dog!
The one and only Willow, the dog!

Katie Simms (10)

My Favourite Person Sam

My neighbour is so cool,
He likes playing football,
His name is Sam,
He loves ham,
His favourite treat is rice pudding and jam,
He loves his rock,
but at thirteen he never changes his sock,
He loves our trampoline,
and looks like a runner bean,
Sam is the best neighbour,
but after this he owes us a favour.

Luca Bartlam (7)

A Friend To Die For

(Dedicated to my late Grandma Nance)

She listens and understands me,
What a fantastic person is she.
She helps me every single day,
In each and every way.
I am proud to say that she is mine,
Because wherever she is, everything is fine.
I love her and she loves me,
What a brilliant pair are we.
For she is my grandma,
And she will always have a place in my heart.

Thomas Clark (11)

My Favourite Person 2009

My favourite person is my sister Aaliyah
My sister is special to me because
Sometimes she makes me laugh
Sometimes she makes me cry
And sometimes she makes me angry
But the special thing about her is
That she will always be there for me
And I will always be there for her
So I hope we will never be afraid to go to each other
When we are in trouble
And I hope we will never grow apart.

Olivia Hooper (10)

The Smile Maker

My baby sister Clara is so cute,
Her eyes are dark chestnut-brown just like mine.
Her hair is soft and curly at the back.
She waddles on her two froggy feet,
Waving to the people she meets.
And when she smiles her two front teeth
Glitter in the summer sun like two diamonds.
It's true she cries sometimes
And wakes me up at night,
And scribbles all over my finished homework!
But she will always be The Smile Maker to me.

Adele Whalley (10)

My Aunt Georgie

My aunt is to me the greatest person in this world,
One of a kind and one in a million.
She has the biggest heart with the most caring touch,
Which she shares with many of us.
In my eyes she will always be
The most beautiful person to walk on Earth.
The memories I will cherish for they are priceless.
For everything she has done, I will forever be thankful,
And my love for her grows more with each day that passes.
She's my favourite aunt in the world
And I am pleased to be related.

Mollie Jenkins (12)

My Mum

My mum is simply the best
heads above the rest
calls me parsnip nose when I'm bold
with her fun and laughter
she never grows old.
In my life I'm loved a lot
but Mum's the one who loves me most
and though I know I shouldn't boast
my mum is the one I love the most
and so this is the reason
for me my mum is my favourite person.

Courtney Louise McCallum (6)

My Sister Amy

My sister, Amy, loves to sing
Acting, dancing and everything
She skips around the house all day
Wondering what she can play.
My sister, Amy, is as bouncy as a bunny
As free as a bee
And as sweet as honey.
My sister, Amy, is great fun
She's very fit and loves to run
That's why Amy is such a good friend
And I'll love her to the very end.

Millie Wood (8)

My Wonderful Mum

She has long red hair,
Twisting, turning, leaping, whirling.
She wears thick gold jewellery,
Emeralds, diamonds, rubies and sapphires.
I love my mum, I always have, I always will.
She loves me when I'm sad
And praises me when I'm good.
I love my mum, I knew I would.
I love my mum, I always have, I always will.
She'll love me through the good times and the bad,
The lonely times and the sad.

Emily Roberts (9)

Jack

My favourite person is Jack,
His least favourite colour is black.
Even though we're cousins,
We're still the best of pals,
We've got each other's backs.
We always disagree on facts.
Even though we have our fights
We take it to the past and move on.
I wrote this poem to show how much I care.
Even if I don't win, I'll treasure a copy forever
To show how much I care about Jack.

Rebecca Williams (10)

My Friend, Fiona

My friend, Fiona, is lovely summery pink,
She is a beautiful hot summer's day at the beach.
My friend, Fiona, is the brightest day of the year,
She is my absolutely favourite jumper
That keeps me warm during the coldest days of winter.
My friend, Fiona, is the comfiest, cosiest chair
In the whole of my house.
She is the most full of life episode of EastEnders ever made.
My friend, Fiona, is the most deliciously flavoured
Apple in the world.
My friend, Fiona, is the best friend I have always wanted.

Rachelle Ogello (11)

My Favourite Person

My favourite person is my big brother Paul.
He's handsome and he's 6 feet tall.
But you know I hardly see him at all.
My big brother Paul is twenty years older than me.
I was a bit of a surprise you see.
He's kind and he's funny and I miss him a lot.
When he comes to see we're out the door in a shot,
Ice skating, swimming and having a laugh
Even though he's as tall as a giraffe.
So my dream for the future would be
That my big brother Paul lived in the house next to me.

Carly Thomson (9)

Special To Me

Here's a poem just for you
About my favourite people.

My dad, well he's a presser,
While my mum, she sometimes cleans.
But they are both accountants
And very, very clean.

Sometimes they are angry,
Sometimes they are not,
But most of all I love them lots
Because they love me back!

Emma Drainey (10)

My Favourite Person Is My Dad

My favourite person is my dad,
except for when he drives me mad.
My favourite person is my dad,
and his real name is Chad.

My favourite person is my dad,
and he has a secret notepad.
My favourite person is my dad,
also he has a friend called Brad.

My favourite person is my dad,
because he never lets me stay sad!

Nailah Khan (11)

Super Sis!

My favourite person is my sister.

S he cares for me
I s always there for me
S he helps me bake cakes
T akes me to the lakes
E ver listening to me deep with interest
R eally, she is truly the best!

When I'm feeling sad,
Simply remember my favourite person,
And then I won't feel so bad.

Chloe Brookes (10)

My Mum

I love my mum and she loves me,
That's why she's always there for me.
We live together in a nice little home,
In our house we don't have garden gnomes.
My mum and I have brown hair and blue eyes,
But my eyes are bigger . . . what a surprise!
My mum is 29 but doesn't look it,
Not too young, she wouldn't fit into my LFC kit.
I love my mum loads and loads,
But even better she loves me loads.

Brooke McCoy (10)

My Brother, Samuel

Samuel, Samuel, my only brother,
He makes me laugh like no other.
Star Wars, Action Men are his things,
But they are not mine, because I like bling.
We both like cats and cars
And for our holiday we would like to visit Mars.
Although my brother is a pain
It simply wouldn't be the same
Without him to play my games.
I love my brother.

Emily Priestley (8)

My Two Friends

My two friends are extraordinary in my home world of England.
One is all about the cool but he isn't rap to rap (not to mention he has
a Mohawk).
The other is as quiet as a chameleon and he is the talk of the school.
But when he is with me he shows his real self
Which is opposite to what people see.
I know I might not be with my fishy friends at the moment
As I am the world away from them
But I know they will always be with me in spirit.
My friends go by the names . . . Max and Ben.

Lekan Olasina (10)

My Favourite Person Is . . .

My favourite person is probably my mum,
Because she is a lot of fun.
Mums tell you right from wrong,
My mum tells me in a song.
Mums wash, cook and clean all day,
I'm very lucky I go out to play.
If I have a problem I'll call my mum,
She will give me advice, no actually a ton.
She is always there for me,
Even when trying to have a cup of tea.

Amy McLean-Nelson (11)

A Boy Called Max

A boy called Max is my best friend.
We play together for hours on end.
We play outside with ball and bat,
(Call the vet, we've hit the cat!)
When indoors we make up games,
If things get broken he gets the blame.
At Christmas time he's full of cheer,
I think he steals Grandad's beer!
We sometimes fight and annoy each other
But we're still best friends, cos he's my brother.

Alex Lowe (11)

My Favourite Feline

My favourite person is my cat,
I hope there's nothing wrong with that,
Pinky Tiger Rambo is his name,
He's very funny and really tame,
His first name is for his nose,
Which is pink as you might suppose,
His second name is for his stripes,
Because like a tiger he often swipes,
His third name comes from our old cat,
Who was hit by a car and squashed quite flat.

Rhys Barnwell (10)

My Best Friend, Socks

My best friend is a dog
And she could jump over a giant log.
Her name is Socks and she is so cool,
She plays with me after school.
Sometimes she rolls over and I tickle her tum,
Her favourite meal is doggy Chum.
She is the best of the whole bunch,
Her favourite thing to do is munch.
Me and Socks will never part,
And she will always be in my heart.

Ella Ross (11)

My Mum

My mum is so fun.
She is an expert at cooking.
My mum is special to me.
She's sometimes not in a good mood.
She helps me for lots of stuff.
My mum's always there for me,
She's very funny and makes me laugh.
I think my mum is important.
My mum's favourite sport is badminton.
That is my mum.

Anisah Shabir (9)

Doug The Dog

My friend Doug
is a very good dog
he loves to play
and run and roll
but most of all
he loves us *all!*

Alex Joseph Gallagher (8)

I Love My Mum

I love my mum, she's my best friend,
She helps me out right to the end.
She's a mixture of good and kind,
Someone like her is hard to find.
I always smile when she's around,
She can turn a frown upside down.
We have such fun when we're together,
She plays with me, whatever the weather.
Sometimes I help my mum cook,
My mum's the best, she rocks!

Izzat Shahzad (10)

My Great Nan

My nan is the best
Walking around in her bright blue vest
I love her so much
Without her I could not live
I see her nearly every day
I think it's best that way
She is the coolest, the prettiest and the kindest
She is number one
No one could beat her
My nan is my lucky charm!

Courtney Wise (11)

My Favourite Person Is My Friend Rebecca

My best friend, Rebecca,
She always makes me smile,
She always makes you laugh,
She's always setting styles.
We love to share a giggle,
We do everything together,
We do it together, whatever the weather!
I have just told you about my friend,
She is the best,
Better than the rest!

Emily Ballentine (11)

Me And My Friend!

My best friend is Caitlin,
We met at playgroup.
She is nice and kind,
Funny and short.
We go to St Joseph's
Since we met again through nursery.
We were friends through the infants
And juniors, sleepovers and parties,
Fallouts and made friends again,
Soon to start high school!

Courtney Donoghue (10)

My Brother Josh

He's like my little shadow, always following me around.
He's always right behind me, whenever I turn around.
I have to take him with me everywhere I go.
I would like some peace and quiet, just to be on my own.
His chatter is incessant, even in his sleep.
Why can't he just be silent and not make a peep?
He wakes early in the morning so full of energy and life.
I just can't help wondering, will I ever be free from strife?
Although he drives me to distraction, I'll defend him to the end.
For I love him, he's my brother and my best friend.

Aaron Dundas (10)

Bounty

Bounty is my rabbit's name,
To jump a fence is his aim.
Snickers is the name of his brother,
You could say I am their mother.
I feed my rabbit every day,
I even give him a bit of hay.
I walk my rabbit on his lead,
And I see to his every need.
My rabbit and I have so much fun,
Especially whilst playing in the sun.

Viktoria Lyon (11)

My Mum

To me my mum is very special,
and in my life she is essential.
With my mum it's so much fun,
she also makes delicious buns.
My mum is so sweet and caring.
She teaches me good lessons in life like sharing.
My mum likes to buy me lots of toys.
She is so proud of me to be her oldest boy.
I'm thankful for her every day.
I hope she never leaves and goes away.

Muhammad Najeeb Hussain (11)

I Love My Cat

I love . . .

I love the way his cotton-soft fur brushes up against my skin.
I love the way his devious little eyes hypnotise me.
I love the way he feels luxurious as he strolls through the room.
I love the way his nurturing little paws tiptoe across the floor.
I love the way he snuggles up at night, warm in his bed.
I love the way he slowly creeps up on his prey
And then he pounces, swooping as fast as lightning!

I love . . . my cat.

Tommy Sizer (11)

My Dad

My dad is the blossom on the tree,
Creating love and laughter throughout me.
He supports and loves me in his own special way
And guides me so that I'm not led astray.
He is cheeky and tickles and is lots of fun,
My dad - he is my number one.
There's no better cuddle
When I'm in a muddle,
That's why I love my dad.

Claire Collins (11)

Roy The Puppy

Roy the boy plays with his toy
Eating it
Ripping it
Chewing it
He's microchipped, goes on walks
And he loves to be near me
He eats his food
He sleeps eventually
It's another day . . .

Jamie Gibson (9)

Patty

Patty is dark brown with a splash of white.
Patty's whiteness is like spilt milk down her fur.
Patty has a long slimy tongue that tickles my face.
She has little eyes that sparkle in the darkness.
Patty's fur is soft as sheep's curly wool.
Patty lies in her bed, looking at me.
She is my best friend!

Alfia Bunyan (9)

My Favourite Person

My favourite person is my gran,
She likes to watch Gok Wan.
She buys me lots of sweets,
Sometimes for a little treat.
She lives in Scotland, far, far away,
We send her texts every day.
She makes me smile
When I haven't seen her for a while.
That's my favourite person!

Vanessa Martin (11)

Milo The Cat

He came from Lincoln
One day in May
And at first he didn't
Want to stay.
He hid in every nook and cranny,
But then he thought everything was funny.
He played with his string
And his little ding-a-ling.
That is why Milo is my very best thing!

Tallulah Kerrigan (9)

Shirley

S hirley!
H appy, funny and generous is my gran
I f I have a frown, she'll act like a clown to make me smile again
R eady to help me whenever I need
L ove is always there for me
E very day is an enjoyable day
Y ou and I make the perfect jigsaw puzzle.

Mackenzie Kellett (10)

My Special Friend

My special friend is called Elizabeth,
She always makes me laugh,
Spaghetti Bolognese is her favourite food
And she's never naughty in class.

She loves to dance, sing and play,
Her favourite colour is pink,
I love to go to her house for tea,
Where I bounce on her trampoline.

Hannah Scarfe (8)

My Favourite People

My favourite person, kind and sweet,
My favourite person, a pleasure to meet,
My favourite person, my bestest friend,
My favourite person, our fun never ends!

My favourite person, it's not the same as last,
My favourite person, whose heart is soft as grass,
My favourite person, who helps me whatever may come,
My favourite person, it's my mum!

Lucas Wong (11)

My Favourite Person - Mum

My mum's my favourite person,
She keeps everything so clean.
My mum's my favourite person,
She's never, ever mean.

She's always there everywhere,
She's always on my mind.
Just remember my mum's the very best,
She never takes a rest from being loving and kind.

Georgie Perry (11)

157

My Grandma, My Friend

I felt her warm breath on my face,
And arms around in warm embrace.
A gentle kiss upon my cheek,
I wanted it to last all week.

This person giving love no end,
My grandma and my special friend.
So let me say, 'Don't let it end.'
Grandma is my special friend.

Ellie Newton (11)

Dad!

My favourite person works all day,
When he comes home we have time to play.
He is really fun and a little bit mad,
His name is Clive and he is my dad!

He likes playing war games with my twin brother,
He takes me riding and so does my mother.
Dad likes to take us to Alton Water,
I hope he thinks I'm number one daughter!

Antonia Morrison (11)

Favourite Person - Mum

Mum is the world's best,
She is better than the rest.
Mum is very smart,
She has got the most tender, loving heart.

We go to the beach and play in the sun,
Mum pulls us around in the boat, we have lots of fun.
She likes her wine while cooking dinner,
That's why my mum should be the number one winner.

James Morrison (11)

158

About My Mum

Who was there when I was born? My mum.
Who fed me when I was a baby? My mum.
My mum taught me how to talk,
My mum taught me how to walk.

My mum is the greatest person to me,
But maybe not to other people.
If my mum never gave birth to me,
I wouldn't be writing this poem.

Fahmid Choudhury (10)

My Magnificent Mum

My mum is the best mum in the world,
Her heart is as pure as gold,
Her smile is very sweet,
And she always gives me a wonderful treat!

My mum has a lot of courage,
She really likes porridge,
I love my mum a lot,
And for my birthday she bought me a toy robot.

Vitesh Dav (10)

Untitled

This is a tale of my best friend
And I will love her till the end
She is quite small but a little chunky
This tale is about Emily my monkey
I've had her now for quite a few years
And if I lose her it brings me to tears
My daddy says she is tailor-made
When I get married she will be my bridesmaid.

Taylor Hartwell (6)

The Mum Poem

Mum is great,
Mum is the best,
When Mum is alone
I always give her a big hug.
When I need Mum,
She is always there.
I love Mum so much.
What would I do without her?

Fazley Luhany (11)

My Mate

My favourite person is my mate,
She helps me in every way,
She always has good things to say.
She's always there for you when you're sad,
She is not a mate that is bad.
My mate is the best,
I will never forget her in my life
Because she's helped me through every way.

Tharsayini Anandaraja (11)

My Best Friend

My best friend is kind and considerate,
Even better than my favourite chocolate.
Although she's very small,
She's got a big heart and big hearts rule.
Cute and cuddly she may be,
If you pick an argument with her, well, you'll see.
There's my best friend, it's as plain as can be,
I'm lucky to have her and she's lucky to have me!

Alice Marriott (10)

My Best Friend

Funny, feisty, fabulous,
Cheerful, cool, cooperative,
Merry, mischievous, marvellous,
Trouble, terrific, talkative,
Silly, sweet, softie,
Exciting, enthusiastic, excellent,
Lovely, lively, loyal,
My best friend!

Noor Majid (11)

Me And The Puppies

I was at school,
when I came home my dog Kim had puppies.
They were small and cute,
I had a look, it was noisy.
Me and the puppies played catchy,
they were it and licked my face.
My uncle has my favourite puppy called Millie.
She is scared of tractor horns so I give her lots of cuddles.

Thomas Leslie (7)

My Great Nan

My great nan is a wonderful lady,
She is 87 years old,
Which makes her very special.
She had 21 children, but only 13 survived!
So my great nan as you can see,
Is very special to me.
She is one in a million
And I love her dearly.

Kayleigh Harris-Pincombe (11)

My Favourite Person

My little sister is called Roisin Anna,
On her birthday we put up a banner.
Sometimes she can be a pickle,
But then laughs when I give her a tickle.
I waited so long for her to arrive,
The day she came home I saw a beehive.
All I ever wanted was a little sister,
Then the next day I got a big blister!

Paige Clowting (8)

My Sister

My sister,
My sister the great,
My sister the great, the caring,
My sister the great, the caring, the beautiful,
My sister the great, the caring, the beautiful, the outgoing,
My sister the great, the caring, the beautiful, the outgoing,
the fun maker,
My sister, my favourite person!

George May (11)

Untitled

Mum is the best of bests,
Although she makes me do the hardest of tests.
She cooks, she cleans -
Even though she's not very keen!
When I want a cuddle,
She gives me a great big huggle.
Mum would never say I'm not clever,
Mum is the best ever!

Ellen Stockley (10)

My Favourite Person

My favourite person is my friend,
Although he drives me round the bend.
We walk to school every day
And always chatter along the way.
His favourite things are footy and sweets,
We play together and share our treats.
There's one last thing I'd like to say,
I'm glad he lives in Whitley Bay.

Ben Thompson (11)

My Mummy

My mummy is so scrummy
and I love her very much,
she is so cute and very funny
and my mummy is the top,
but she does not go pop!
I love her very much
because she is my mummy,
my mummy! *Hooray!*

Emily Watkins (8)

My Favourite Person

My favourite person is Joshua Haynes,
he likes playing games,
me and Joshua are the same,
we like playing games,
we share the same name Joshua,
me and Joshua are special friends,
we are both 6 years old and we
think we are as good as gold.

Joshua Garbett (6)

My Big Brother

My brother Ty
Is my favourite, should I tell you why?
He's tall and thin,
I could throw him like a javelin,
He's very funny,
He gives me sweets and he gives me money,
He would stick up for me if I needed a hand,
He is my favourite in the whole, entire land!

Tori Creighton (10)

My Favourite Person
Is My Older Cousin, Jay

His favourite day's when I come and play,
He always has a lot to say!
When we go to Nana's house we play all day,
He likes his Game Boy, it is his favourite toy.
He has got a pet called Lunar, that's a dog
And she jumps around as if she were a frog!

Oliver Grant (9)

Mum, Mum

Mum, Mum makes me smile,
Mum, Mum makes me laugh,
Mum, Mum loves me a lot,
Mum, Mum is the best,
Mum, Mum I love you,
Mum, Mum you are the number one.
I love you.

Nora Mwakatuma (9)

My Brother Krrish

K ing of his lair
R uler of his room
R ummaging about everywhere
I nch by inch aiming for the moon
S earching, crawling around
H iding all about . . .
    The only time Krrish will come out is when it's cartoon time!

Shaneel Mungul (10)

Grandad

G rey hair, but still fun, even if there is something wrong
R eady to go if I am slow to come to pick me up to go
A lready here and full of go, anywhere I want to go
N ever late to go to town to buy me a new dressing gown
D ry day in town today, ready to stay for the day
A lways waiting patiently as shop to shop we wander
D riving home tired but happy, just in time for dinner.

Ceirios Thomas (8)

About Mum

My mum smiles at me when it rains,
She smells like roses on a summer's day.
We play in the snow all day.
My mum reminds me of the birds whistling in the morning.
My mum's like a teddy giving me hugs and kisses at night.
Sometimes my mum gives me breakfast in bed.
I love my mum!

Ellie Johnson (10)

My Favourite

On my bed he sleeps

Under my quilt he creeps

He's always there . . .

My favourite person is

My brown bear.

Ellie Price (10)

Who Is It?

My favourite person is very nice,
My favourite person likes to chase mice,
My favourite person is black and white,
My favourite person is fluffy and light.
Have you guessed who it is?
It's my cat!

Cassidy Robertson (11)

My Dog, Jack

My dog, Jack,
Likes to lie on his back.
He likes me to tickle his tummy
And likes to go for long walks when it's sunny.
Jack loves to sleep on my bed,
I wish he would sleep in his own bed instead!

Adam Dennis (11)

My Guardian Angel

Lilac is her name and hockey is her game,
She loves tennis but she is not a menace,
She has been a nan
Although other people would call it a gran,
She never whines and she never moans,
But everyone says she isn't stuck up her nose!

Erica Constantine (11)

My Cat

I am Kerry and I have a cat.
She rather likes to sit on the mat.
When you walk past she purrs with delight.
And when you play a game she tries to win with great might.
My cat is called Penny and she eats quite a lot.
And sometimes she takes a lot of thought.

Kerry Halpin (9)

My Friend Imogen

Is one of a kind, she's pretty hard to find.
With her blonde hair, a funny smile,
She'll be here for a while.
Plus with her wink you'll just sink.
There are so many spaces to spare, it's that easy to pair.
This is no joke, by the way she loves Coke.

Miles Beard (8)

Friend By Whisker

Cuthbert is my tabby cat,
He loves to play around,
Whacking leaves up and down
And creeping about without a sound.
My cat loves to eat meat and chicken strips.
He is a healthy eater, 'cause he doesn't like chips!

Aiden Neale (9)

Young Writers Information

We hope you have enjoyed reading this
book - and that you will continue to enjoy it
in the coming years.

If you like reading and writing poetry drop us
a line, or give us a call, and we'll send you a
free information pack.

Alternatively if you would like to order further
copies of this book or any of our other titles, then
please give us a call or log onto our website at
www.youngwriters.co.uk

Young Writers Information
Remus House
Coltsfoot Drive
Peterborough
PE2 9JX
(01733) 890066